GLOBETROTTER

G000077767

LATIN AMERICAN
SPANISH
In Your Pocket

NEW
HOLLAND

GLOBETROTTER™

First edition published in 2007
by New Holland Publishers Ltd
London • Cape Town • Sydney
• Auckland
10 9 8 7 6 5 4 3 2 1

www.newhollandpublishers.com

Garfield House, 86 Edgware Road
London W2 2EA
United Kingdom

80 McKenzie Street
Cape Town 8001
South Africa

14 Aquatic Drive
Frenchs Forest, NSW 2086
Australia

218 Lake Road
Northcote, Auckland
New Zealand

Copyright © 2007 in text:
José Hares
Copyright © 2007 in photograph:
Pictures Colour Library
Copyright © 2007 in illustrations:
Marisa Galloway
Copyright © 2007 New Holland
Publishers (UK) Ltd

ISBN 978 1 84537 809 7

Although every effort has been made
to ensure that this guide is correct at
time of going to print, the Publisher
accepts no responsibility or liability for
any loss, injury or inconvenience
incurred by readers or travellers
using this guide.

Publishing Manager:
Thea Grobbelaar
Cover design: Nicole Bannister
Designer: Lellyn Creamer
Illustrator: Marisa Galloway
Editor: Thea Grobbelaar
Translator: José Hares
Consultant: Lynn Zinn

Reproduction by Resolution, Cape Town
Printed and bound by
Replika Press Pvt Ltd, India

Cover photograph: *La Boca El
Caminito, Buenos Aires, Argentina.*

CONTENTS

This PHRASE BOOK is thematically colour-coded for easy use and is organized according to the situation you're most likely to be in when you need it. The fairly comprehensive DICTIONARY section consists of two parts – English/Spanish and Spanish/English.

To make speaking Spanish easy, we encourage our readers to memorize some general PRONUNCIATION rules (*see* page 8). After you have familiarized yourself with the basic tools of the language and the rudiments of Spanish GRAMMAR (see page 14), all you need to do is turn to the appropriate section of the phrase book and find the words you need to make yourself understood. If the selection is not exactly what you're looking for, consult the dictionary for other options.

Just to get you started, here are some Spanish expressions you might have heard, read or used at some time: *adiós, por favor, gracias, hasta mañana, siesta.* Even if you are unfamiliar with these words and would rather not try to say them out loud, just remain confident, follow our easy advice and practise a little, and you will soon master useful phrases for everyday life. Speak slowly and enunciate carefully and your counterpart is likely to follow suit.

Some Spanish words, especially those ending in -ion, are pronounced differently from their English equivalents (e.g. extensión – *ex-ten-syon*), or else changed just slightly (mayonnaise – *mayonesa*), though their meanings remain clear. Nowadays many English terms are used in Spanish, especially in business, sport and leisure activities, so everyone will know what you mean when you say things like 'laptop', 'golf' and 'tennis'.

A section on HOLIDAYS AND FESTIVALS (*see* page 82) provides some background knowledge so that you know what you're celebrating and why. There's no better way to learn a language than joining in some enjoyment!

The brief section on manners, mannerisms and ETIQUETTE (*see* page 76) can help you make sense of the people around you. Make an effort to view your host country and its people tolerantly – that way you will be open to the new experience and able to enjoy it.

Learning a new language can be a wonderful but frightening experience. It is not the object of this book to teach you perfect Spanish, but rather to equip you with just enough knowledge for a successful holiday or business trip. Luckily you are unlikely to be criticized on your grammatical correctness when merely asking for directions. The most important thing is to make yourself understood. To this end a brief section on grammar and a guide to pronunciation have been included in this book. There is, however, no substitute for listening to native speakers.

Before you leave, it might be a good idea to familiarize yourself with the sections on Pronunciation, Grammar and Etiquette. This can easily be done en route to your destination. You will also benefit from memorizing a few important phrases before you go.

The sections of the Phrase Book are arranged by topic for quick reference. Simply go to the contents list (*see* page 3) to find the topic you need. The Dictionary section (*see* page 88) goes both ways, helping you to understand and be understood.

Abbreviations have been used where one English word could be interpreted as more than one part of speech, e.g. 'smoke' (a noun, the substance coming from a fire) and 'smoke' (a verb, what one would do with a cigarette). Here is a list of these and some other abbreviations used in this book:

vb	verb
n	noun
adj	adjective
adv	adverb
prep	preposition
pol	polite
fam	familiar (informal)
elec	electric/al
med	medical
anat	anatomy
rel	religion
Lat Am	Latin America/n
Sp	Spain

The gender and number of Spanish nouns have been specified as follows:

m	masculine
f	feminine
pl	plural

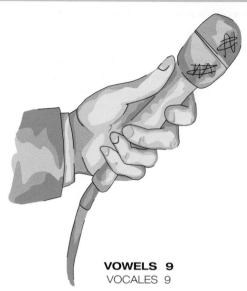

Spanish is a phonetic language, so with a bit of practice you can soon read most of it. Many letters are pronounced much like the English equivalent. The English words given here contain sounds that approximate Spanish sounds.

VOWELS
VOCALES

♦ **a** – like the **a** in father – *gato*
♦ **e** – like the **e** in let – *me*
♦ **i** – like the **ee** in meet – *hijo*
♦ **o** – like the **o** in order – *yo*
♦ **u** – like the **oo** in foot, but shorter – *tu*

NB The letter **u** following a **g** or a **q** is silent, unless marked with an umlaut – *desagüe*.

DIPHTHONGS
DIPTONGOS

♦ **ai** – like the **i** in bite – *bailar*
♦ **ay** – like the **i** in bite – *hay*
♦ **au** – like the **ow** in cow – *audiencia*
♦ **ei** – like the **ey** in they – *reina*
♦ **ey** – like the **ey** in they – *ley*
♦ **eu** – sound each vowel separately – *Europa*
♦ **ia** – like the **ya** in yard – *enviar*

- **ie** – like the **ye** in **yes** – *tiene*
- **io** – like the **yo** in **yo**re – *junio*
- **iu** – like **you** – *viuda*
- **oi** – like the **oy** in **toy** – *boicot*
- **oy** – like the **oy** in **toy** – *estoy*
- **ua** – like the **wa** in **want** – *cuando*
- **uay** – like the **wi** in **wise** – *Uruguay*
- **ue** – like the **wea** in **weather** – *bueno*
- **uey** – like the **wai** in **wait** – *buey*
- **ui** – like the **wee** in **week** – *suizo*
- **uo** – like the **wo** in **woke** – *cuota*

If a vowel is marked with an accent (e.g. é, á), it indicates that this syllable is stressed.

CONSONANTS
CONSONANTES

- **b** – see **v**
- **c** – like the **k** in **keep** – *cabeza*
- **c** – before **e** and **i**, like the **s** in **site**
- **ch** – like the **ch** in **chop** – *mucho*
- **d** – between vowels or at the end of a word, it sounds like the **th** in **father** – *cada*
- **g** – before **e** and **i**, it sounds like the **ch** in **loch** (represented as **kh** in this book) – *gente*
- **g** – like the **g** in **get** – *gato*

- **h** – the letter **h** is always silent – *hola*
- **j** – like the **ch** in lo**ch** (represented as **kh** in this book) – *jueves*
- **ll** – in Argentina and Uruguay, a soft **sh** sound, like the **g** in beige (or, in Spain, like the **y** in yet) – *silla*
- **ñ** – like the **ny** in ca**ny**on – *niño*
- **q** – like the **c** in car – *querer*
- **r** – rolled as in Scots – *pero*
- **rr** – a lengthened rolled **r** sound – *perro*
- **s** – always pronounced like the **s** in **s**oap, never like the **s** in ea**s**y – *mesa*
- **v** – like a cross between the English **b** and **v** (with the lips barely meeting) – *mover*
- **z** – like the **s** in **s**ite – *azul*

There are variations in the pronunciation of Spanish, depending on where it is spoken, for example in Latin America, Andalucía or the rest of Spain. For example, the letter **z**, when spoken by the people in Latin America, would sound like the **s** in **s**imple, whereas in Spain it would be pronounced like the **th** in **th**ing. Wherever you are, you will soon know how to pronounce the words simply by listening to the local people speaking.

Practise a few phrases in Spanish (the stressed syllables are underlined:

Buenos días
bwe-nos dee-yas
Good day

¡Hola!
o-la
Hello!

Adiós
ad-yos
Goodbye

¿Habla inglés?
ab-la in-gless
Do you speak English?

Hable despacio, por favor
ab-leh des-paa-syoh, por fa-vor
Please speak slowly

No entiendo
noh ent-yen-doh
I don't understand

¿Cómo está usted?
koh-moh es-ta oos-ted
How are you? (polite)

¿Qué tal?
keh tal
How are you? (familiar)

Bien, gracias
byen, graa-syass
Fine, thanks!

Quiero ...
kyeh-roh
I'd like ...

¿Cómo dice?
ko-mo dee-seh
Pardon?

Por favor
por fa-vor

¡Gracias!
graa-syass
Thank you!

¡Lo siento!
  (¡Disculpe!)
loh syen-toh
  (dis-cool-peh)
Sorry! Excuse me!

¿Dónde está el
  baño?
don-deh es-tah
  el banyo
Where is the toilet?

¿Cuándo llega el
  tren?
kwan-doh yeh-gah
  el trenn
When does the train
  arrive?

¿Dónde está?
don-deh es-tah
Where is it?

¿Puedo ...?
pweh-doh
May I ...?

ayer
ah-yehr
yesterday

hoy
oy
today

mañana
ma-nya-na
tomorrow

¿Puedo llamar por
  teléfono?
pweh-doh yah-mahr
  por te-leh-foh-noh
May I use the phone?

The grammar section has deliberately been kept very brief as this is not a language course.

PERSONAL PRONOUNS
PRONOMBRES PERSONALES

Subject	
yo	I
tú	you (fam)
usted (ud.)	you (pol)
él, ella	he/she
nosotros/as	we
ustedes (uds.)	you (pl – Lat Am)
vosotros/as	you (pl – Spain)
ellos/ellas	they

Direct Object		Indirect Object	
me	me	(to) me	me
you	te (fam)	(to) you	te (fam)
you	le (pol)	(to) you	le (pol)
him	le	(to) him	le
her	la	(to) her	le
it	lo	(to) it	le
us	nos	(to) us	nos
you	les (pl – Lat. Am)	(to) you	les (pl – Lat Am)
you	os (pl – Spain)	(to) you	os (pl – Spain)
them	les	(to) them	les

Reflexive Pronoun

myself	me
yourself	te (fam)
yourself	se (pol)
himself	se
herself	se
itself	se
ourselves	nos
yourselves	se (pl – Lat Am)
yourselves	os (pl – Spain)
themselves	se

Possessive Pronoun

mine	mío/a
yours	tuyo/a (fam)
yours	suyo/a (pol)
his	suyo/a, suyos/as, de él
hers	suyo/a, suyos/as, de ella
its	suyo/a, suyos/as
ours	nuestro/a, nuestros/as
yours	vuestro/a, vuestros/as (pl – Spain)
yours	suyo/a, suyos/as (pl – Lat Am)
theirs	suyo/a, suyos/as

The gender of a pronoun refers to the gender of the object you are talking about, and not to your own gender. Whether you yourself are male or female, you would say the book (masculine) is mine (*el libro es mío*), or the house (feminine) is mine (*la casa es mía*).

When referring to parts of your body, the possessive pronoun is not used – you would say 'the leg' (*la pierna*) rather than 'my leg' (*mí pierna*)

VERBS
VERBOS

All verbs in their infinitive form end in -ar, -er or -ir. Each verb has a stem or a root and an appropriate ending (be it -ar, -er or -ir). The stem of the verb is the part that precedes the ending. For example, the verb *cantar* (to sing) can be broken up as follows: *cant-* (root) and -*ar* (ending).

The verbs that never change their stem and follow conjugation patterns are called *regulares* (about 75% of verbs), and the ones that change stem are called *irregulares* (about 25%).

Examples of REGULAR verbs, present tense:

AMAR (to love)
yo amO
tú amAS
él/ella/usted amA
nosotros amAMOS
vosotros amÁIS (Sp)
ellos/ustedes amAN

TEMER (to fear)
yo temO
tú temES
él/ella/usted temE
nosotros temEMOS
vostros temÉIS (Sp)
ellos/ustedes temEN

PARTIR (to leave)
yo partO
tú partES
él/ella/usted partE
nosotros partIMOS
vosotros partÍS (Sp)
ellos/ustedes partEN

Here are some useful IRREGULAR verbs:

TENER (to have)
yo tengo
tú tienes
él/ella/usted tiene
nosotros tenemos
vosotros tenéis (Sp)
ellos/ustedes tienen

QUERER (to want)
yo quiero
tú quieres
él/ella/usted quiere
nosotros queremos
vosotros queréis (Sp)
ellos/ustedes quieren

IR (to go)
yo voy
tú vas
él/ella/usted va
nosotros vamos
vosotros vais (Sp)
ellos/ustedes van

PODER (can)
you puedo
tú puedes
él/ella/usted puede
nosotros podemos
vosotros podéis (Sp)
ellos/ustedes pueden

SER (to be)
yo soy
tú eres
él/ella/usted es
nosotros somos
vosotros sois (Sp)
ellos/ustedes son

ESTAR (to be)
yo estoy
tú estás
él/ella/usted está

ESTAR (continued)
nosotros estamos,
vosotros estáis (Sp)
ellos/ustedes están

HACER (to make/do)
yo hago
tú haces
él/ella/usted hace
nosotros hacemos
vosotros hacéis (Sp)
ellos/ustedes hacen

DECIR (to say)
yo digo
tú dices
él/ella/usted dice
nosotros decimos
vosotros decís (Sp)
ellos/ustedes dicen

NOUNS – SUSTANTIVOS

Nouns ending in -**o** are usually masculine and
nouns ending in -**a** are usually feminine. To form
the plural, add -**s** if the noun ends in a vowel
and -**es** if the noun ends in a consonant.

ARTICLES – ARTÍCULOS

Definite Article (Artículo Definido) – **the**

el	(masc. sing.)	*la*	(fem. sing.)
los	(masc. pl.)	*las*	(fem. pl.)

Examples:

el libro (the book)   *la casa* (the house)
los libros (the books)   *las casas* (the houses)

Indefinite Article (Artículo Indefinido) – **a, some**

un	(masc. sing.)	*una*	(fem. sing.)
unos	(masc. pl.)	*unas*	(fem. pl.)

Examples:

un perro (a dog)   *una planta* (a plant)
unos perros (some dogs) *unas plantas*
                             (some plants)

ADJECTIVES – ADJETIVOS

Adjectives usually follow the nouns they qualify
(*un libro nuevo* – a new book). Most adjectives
have a masculine and a feminine form (red –
(*rojo/roja*) as well as a singular and plural form
(red – *rojos/rojas*). All adjectives agree in gender and number with the nouns they qualify.
Adjectives not ending in -o or -a do not change

into the masculine or feminine form, but do change to form plurals (*la casa grande* – the big house; *las casas grandes* – the big houses).

PUNCTUATION
PUNTUACIÓN

You may have noticed the upside-down questions marks and exclamation marks used on page 12. In Spanish, a question is introduced by such an upside-down question mark, and concluded with a 'right-way-up' question mark as we know it in English. The same is true of the exclamation mark.

WORD ORDER
ORDEN DE LAS PALABRAS

Spanish word order will probably seem strange to English ears. The adjective usually comes after the noun it modifies (see page 20), but quantifying adjectives usually precede the noun (many books – *muchos libros*). The adjective also precedes the noun if you want to emphasize the adjective rather than the noun.

A question usually has exactly the same word order as a statement, but is distinguished from a statement by the two question marks.

NUMBERS
NÚMEROS

0	cero (*seh*-roh)
1	uno (*oo*-noh)
2	dos (*doss*)
3	tres (*tress*)
4	cuatro (*kwat*-roh)
5	cinco (*seeng*-koh)
6	seis (*sayss*)
7	siete (*s'yet*-teh)
8	ocho (*ot*-choh)
9	nueve (*nweh*-veh)
10	diez (*d'yess*)
11	once (*on*-seh)
12	doce (*doh*-seh)
13	trece (*treh*-seh)
14	catorce (kah-*torr*-seh)
15	quince (*keen*-seh)
16	dieciséis (d'yes-ee-*sayss*)
17	diecisiete (d'yes-ee-*s'yet*-teh)
18	dieciocho (d'yes-ee-*ot*-choh)
19	diecinueve (d'yes-ee-*nweh*-veh)
20	veinte (*bayn*-teh)
21	veintiuno (*bayn*-tee-*oo*-noh)
22	veintidós (*bayn*-tee-*doss*)
30	treinta (*trayn*-ta)
31	treinta y uno (*trayn*-ta-ee-*oo*-noh)
40	cuarenta (kwa-*ren*-ta)
50	cincuenta (seeng-*kwen*-ta)
60	sesenta (seh-*sen*-ta)
70	setenta (seh-*ten*-ta)
80	ochenta (otch-*en*-ta)
90	noventa (noh-*ven*-ta)
100	cien (*s'yen*)
101	ciento uno (*s'yen*-toh-*oo*-noh)
120	ciento viente (*s'yen*-toh-*bayn*-teh)
200	doscientos (doss-*s'yen*-toss)
500	quinientos (keen-*yen*-toss)
1000	mil (*meel*)
1 million	un millón (oon mee-*yon*)
1 billion	un billón (oon bee-*yon*)

DAYS DÍAS	**MONTHS** MESES

DAYS
DÍAS

Monday
lunes (*loo*-ness)

Tuesday
martes (*marr*-tess)

Wednesday
miércoles
(*m'yehr*-koh-less)

Thursday
jueves (*khweh*-vess)

Friday
viernes (*b'yer*-ness)

Saturday
sábado (*sabba*-doh)

Sunday
domingo
(doh-*meeng*-goh)

weekdays
días de semana (*dee*-yass deh seh-*ma*-na)

weekends
fines de semana (*fee*-ness deh seh-*ma*-na)

public holidays
feriados (ferr-*ya*-doss)

MONTHS
MESES

January
enero (eh-*neh*-roh)

February
febrero (feb-*reh*-roh)

March
marzo (*marr*-soh)

April
abril (ab-*reel*)

May
mayo (*ma*-yoh)

June
junio (*khoon*-yoh)

July
julio (*khool*-yoh)

August
agosto (*agoss*-toh)

September
setiembre (set-*yem*-breh)

October
octubre (ok-*too*-breh)

November
noviembre
(nov-*yem*-breh)

24

December
diciembre
(dees-yem-breh)

TIME
LA HORA

in the morning
por la mañana
(porr la man-ya-na)

in the afternoon
por la tarde
(porr la tarr-deh)

in the evening
por la noche
(por la notche)

What is the time?
¿Qué hora es?
(keh oh-ra ess)

* **it's one o'clock**
* es la una *(ess la oo-na)*

* **it's quarter to three**
* son las tres menos
  cuarto *(son lass tress
  mennos kwarr-toh)*

* **it's half past two**
* son las dos y media
  *(son lass doss ee
  med-ya)*

* **twenty past two**
* son las dos y veinte
  *(son lass doss ee
  bayn-teh)*

* **early**
* temprano *(tem-pra-noh)*

* **late**
* tarde *(tarr-deh)*

at 10 a.m. (10:00)
a las diez de la mañana
*(allas d'yess della
man-ya-na)*

at 5 p.m. (17:00)
a las cinco de la tarde
*(allas seeng-koh della
tarr-deh)*

at 9 p.m. (21:00)
a las nueve de la noche
*(allas nweh-veh della
notcheh)*

day after tomorrow
pasado mañana
(pa-saa-doh man-ya-na)

day before yesterday
anteayer *(anteh-a-yerr)*

this morning
esta mañana
(ess-ta man-ya-na)

yesterday evening
ayer por la noche/tarde
(a-<u>yerr</u> porr la <u>no</u>tcheh/<u>tarr</u>-deh)

tomorrow morning
mañana por la mañana
(man-<u>ya</u>-na porr la man-<u>ya</u>-na)

last night
anoche
(a-<u>no</u>tcheh)

this week
esta semana
(ess-ta seh-<u>ma</u>-na)

next week
la semana próxima
(la seh-<u>ma</u>-na <u>prok</u>-see-ma)

now
ahora
(a-<u>oh</u>-ra)

What is today's date?
¿Qué día es hoy?
(keh <u>dee</u>-ya ess <u>oy</u>)

It's 4 June
Es el cuatro de junio
(ess ell <u>kwat</u>-roh de <u>khoon</u>-yoh)

GREETINGS
SALUDOS

Good morning
Buenos días
(<u>bwenn</u>oss <u>dee</u>-yass)

Good afternoon
Buenas tardes
(<u>bwenn</u>ass <u>tarr</u>-dess)

Good evening
Buenas tardes/noches
(<u>bwenn</u>ass <u>tarr</u>-dess/<u>no</u>tchess)

Good night
Buenas noches
(<u>bwenn</u>ass <u>no</u>tchess)

Hello
Hola *(<u>Olla</u>)*

Goodbye
Adiós *(ad-<u>yoss</u>)*

Cheerio
Chau *(chow)*

See you soon
Hasta pronto
(<u>ass</u>-ta <u>pron</u>-toh)

See you later
Hasta luego
(<u>ass</u>-ta <u>lwe</u>-goh)

Have a good time
Que te diviertas/que la pases bien *(keh teh deev-yehr-tass/ keh la passess byen)*

I have to go now
Debo irme ahora *(deb-boh eer-meh a-oh-ra)*

It was very nice
Fue muy agradable *(fweh mooee agra-da-bleh)*

My name is ...
Mi nombre es ... *(mee nom-breh ess ...)*

What is your name?
¿Cómo se llama? (pol) *(kom-moh seh yaa-ma)*
¿Cómo te llamas? (fam) *(kom-moh teh yaa-mass)*

Pleased to meet you!
¡Mucho gusto! *(moo-choh goos-toh)*

How are you?
¿Cómo está? (pol) *(kom-moh ess-ta)*
¿Que tal? (fam) *(keh tal)*

Fine, thanks. And you?
Bien, gracias. ¿Y usted? (pol) *(byen graas-yass, ee oos-ted)*

GENERAL
GENERALES

Do you speak English?
¿Hablas inglés? *(ab-las eeng-gless)*

I don't understand
No comprendo/ no entiendo *(noh kom-pren-doh/noh ent-yen-doh)*

Please speak slowly
Por favor, habla despacio *(por fa-vor, ab-la des-pa-s'yoh)*

Please repeat that
Por favor, repite eso *(por fa-vor, reh-pee-teh essoh)*

Please write it down
Por favor, escríbelo *(por fa-vor, es-cree-beh-loh)*

Excuse me please
Discúlpame/perdóname *(dees-cool-pa-meh/ per-donna-meh)*

Could you help me?
¿Me puedes ayudar? *(meh pweh-dess a-yoo-darr)*

27

Could you do me a favour?
¿Puedes hacerme un favor? (*pweh*-dess a-*serr*-meh oon fa-*vor*)

Can you show me?
¿Puedes mostrarme? (*pweh*-dess moss-*trarr*-meh)

how?
¿cómo? (*kom*-moh)

where?
¿dónde? (*donn*-deh)

when?
¿cuándo? (*kwan*-doh)

who?
¿quién? (*k'yen*)

why?
¿por qué? (porr *keh*)

which?
¿cuál? (*kwal*)

I need ...
necesito ... (ne-seh-*see*-toh ...)

yes
sí (*see*)

no
no (*noh*)

FORMS & SIGNS
IMPRESOS & SIGNOS

Please complete in block letters
Rellene con mayúsculas de imprenta, por favor (reh-*yen*-neh con ma-*yoos*-cool-las deh eem-*pren*-ta, por fa-*vor*)

Surname
Apellido (appeh-*yee*-doh)

First names
Nombres (*nom*-bress)

Date of birth
Fecha de nacimiento (*fetcha* deh nasee-*m'yen*-toh)

Place of birth
Lugar de nacimiento (*loo*-garr deh nasee-*m'yen*-toh)

Occupation
Profesión (proh-fes-*s'yon*)

Nationality
Nacionalidad (na-s'yoh-nalli-*dad*)

Address
Dirección (dee-rec-*s'yon*)

Date of arrival
Fecha de llegada (_fetcha deh yeg-ga-da_)

Date of departure
Fecha de partida (_fetcha deh parr-tee-dah_)

Passport number
Número de pasaporte (_noo-meh-roh deh passa-por-teh_)

I.D. number
Número de documento de identidad (_noo-meh-roh deh dok-oo-men-toh deh ee-dentee-dad_)

Issued at
Expedido en (_expeh-dee-doh en_)

Engaged, Vacant
Ocupado, Libre (_okkoo-pa-doh, lee-breh_)

No trespassing
No pasar (_noh pas-sarr_)

Out of order
No funciona (_noh foon-s'yoh-na_)

Please don't disturb
Por favor, no moleste (_por fa-vor, noh moh-less-teh_)

Push, Pull
Empuje, Tire (_em-poo-kheh, tee-reh_)

Adults and children
Adultos y niños (_a-dool-toss ee neen-yoss_)

Lift/Elevator
Ascensor/Elevador (_as-senn-sorr/ele-va-dorr_)

Escalator
Escalera mecánica (_es-ca-leh-ra meh-ka-nee-ka_)

Wet paint
Pintura fresca (_peen-too-ra fress-ka_)

Open, Closed
Abierto, Cerrado (_ab'yer-toh, ser-ra-doh_)

Till/Cash Desk
Caja (_ka-kha_)

Opening hours
Horario de trabajo (_or-raar-yoh deh tra-ba-khoh_)

Self-service
Autoservicio (_aoo-toh-serr-vee-s'yoh_)

Waiting Room
Sala de espera (_sa-la deh ess-peh-rah_)

BUS STOP
PARADA DE AUTOBÚS

Where is the bus stop?
¿Dónde está la parada de autobús?
(Donn-deh ess-ta la pa-ra-da deh aoo-toh-booss)

Which bus do I take?
¿Cuál autobús debo tomar? *(Kwal aoo-toh-booss debboh toh-marr)*

How often do the buses go?
¿Con qué frecuencia pasan los buses? *(Kon keh freh-kwens-ya pas-san loss booss-ess)*

When is the last bus?
¿A qué hora pasa el ultimo autobús? *(A keh oh-ra passa ell ool-tee-moh aoo-toh-booss)*

Which ticket must I buy?
¿Cuál billete debo comprar? *(Kwal bee-yet-teh debboh kom-prarr)*

Where must I go?
¿Dónde debo ir?
(Donn-deh debboh eer)

I want to go to ....
Quiero ir a...
(K'yeh-roh eer a ...)

What is the fare to...?
¿Cuánto cuesta a ...?
(Kwan-toh kwess-ta a ...)

When is the next bus?
¿En cuánto tiempo llegará el próximo autobús?
(En kwan-toh t'yem-poh yegga-ra ell prok-see-moh aoo-toh-booss)

UNDERGROUND/ SUBWAY/METRO
METRO/ SUBTERRÁNEO

entrance, exit
entrada, salida
(en-tra-da, sa-lee-da)

inner zone, outer zone
zona interna, zona externa
(soh-na een-terr-na, soh-na ex-terr-na)

Where is the under-ground/subway station?
¿Dónde está la estación de metro? *(Donn-deh ess-ta la es-ta-s'yon deh met-roh)*

Do you have a map for the metro?
¿Tiene un mapa para el metro? *(T'yen-neh oon mappa parra ell met-roh)*

I want to go to ....
Quiero ir a...
(K'yeh-roh eer a ...)

Can you give me change?
¿Puede cambiarme/darme cambio? *(Pweh-deh kam-b'yarr-meh/darr-meh kam-b'yoh)*

Which ticket must I buy?
¿Cuál billete debo comprar? *(Kwal bee-yet-teh debboh kom-prarr)*

When is the next train?
¿En cuánto tiempo llegará el próximo tren? *(En kwan-toh t'yem-poh yegga-ra ell prok-see-moh trenn)*

TRAIN/RAILWAY
TREN/FERROCARRIL

Where is the railway station?
¿Dónde está la estación de tren? *(Donn-deh ess-ta la es-ta-s'yon deh trenn)*

departure
salidas *(sa-lee-dass)*

arrival
llegadas *(yeg-ga-dass)*

Which platform?
¿Cuál andén?
(Kwal an-den)

Do you have a timetable?
¿Tiene un horario? *(T'yen-neh oon or-raar-yoh)*

A ... ticket please
Un billete ... por favor
(Oon bee-yet-teh ... por fa-vor)

◆ **single**
◆ ida *(ee-da)*

◆ **return**
◆ ida y vuelta
(ee-da ee bwel-ta)

- **child's**
- infantil (*een-fan-teel*)

- **first class**
- primera clase
  (*pree-meh-ra kla-seh*)

- **second class**
- segunda clase
  (*seh-goon-da kla-seh*)

- **smoking**
- fumador (*foo-ma-dorr*)

- **non-smoking**
- no fumador (*noh foo-ma-dorr*)

Do I have to pay a supplement?

¿Debo pagar exceso? (*Debboh pa-garr ex-sessoh*)

Is my ticket valid on this train?

¿Mi billete es válido en este tren? (*Mee bee-yet-teh ess ba-lee-doh en ess-teh trenn*)

Where do I have to get off?

¿Dónde debo bajarme? (*Donn-deh debboh ba-khar-meh*)

I want to book ...

Quiero reservar ...
(*K'yeh-roh reh-ser-varr ...*)

- **a seat**
- un asiento
  (*oon ass-yen-toh*)

- **a couchette**
- un coche cama
  (*oon kotcheh ca-ma*)

Is this seat free?

¿Este asiento está ocupado? (*Ess-teh ass-yen-toh ess-ta okkoo-pa-doh*)

That is my seat

Ese es mi asiento
(*Es-seh ess mee ass-yen-toh*)

May I open (close) the window?

¿Puedo abrir (cerrar) la ventana? (*Pweh-doh ab-reer [ser-rarr] la ben-ta-na*)

Where is the restaurant car?

¿Dónde está el coche comedor? (*Donn-deh ess-ta ell kotcheh kommeh-dorr*)

Is there a sleeper?
¿Hay un coche cama?
*(Aee oon kotcheh
ca-ma)*

IC – Intercity
Luxury international
express, supplement
payable

stationmaster
jefe de estación
*(khef-feh deh
ess-ta-s'yon)*

BOATS
BARCOS

cruise
crucero *(kroo-seh-roh)*

Can we hire a boat?
¿Podemos alquilar una
lancha?
*(Poh-deh-moss
al-kee-larr oona lan-chah)*

**How much is a
round trip?**
¿Cuánto cuesta un viaje
de ida y vuelta?
*(Kwan-toh kwes-ta oon
b'ya-kheh deh ee-da ee
bwel-ta)*

one ticket
un billete
(oon bee-yet-teh)

two tickets
dos billetes
(doss bee-yet-tess)

**Can we eat on
board?**
¿Se puede comer a
bordo?
*(Seh pweh-deh ko-merr
a borr-doh)*

**When is the last
boat?**
¿A qué hora sale el
último lancha?
*(A keh oh-ra sa-leh
ell ool-tee-moh
lan-chah)*

**When is the next
ferry?**
¿A qué hora sale la
próxima barca/
transbordador?
*(A keh oh-ra sa-leh la
prok-see-ma barr-ka/
trans-borda-dorr)*

**How long does the
crossing take?**
¿Cuánto tarda el cruce?
*(Kwan-toh tarr-da ell
kroo-seh)*

Is the sea rough?
¿El mar está bravo?
(Ell marr ess-ta bra-voh)

TAXI
TAXI

Please order me a taxi
Por favor, llame un taxi (Por fa-_vor_, _ya_-meh oon _ta_xi)

Where can I get a taxi?
¿Dónde puedo tomar un taxi? (_Donn_-deh _pweh_-doh toh-_marr_ oon _ta_xi)

To this address, please
A esta dirección, por favor (A _ess_-ta dee-rek-s'yon, por fa-_vor_)

How much is it to the centre?
¿Cuánto cuesta al centro de la ciudad?(_Kwan_-toh _kwess_-ta al _sen_-troh della see-oo-_dad_)

To the airport, please
Al aeropuerto, por favor (Al a-ehroh-_pwerr_-toh, por fa-_vor_)

To the station, please
A la estación, por favor (Alla es-ta-s'_yon_ por fa-_vor_)

Keep the change
Quédese con el cambio (_Keh_-deh-seh kon ell _kam_-b'yoh)

I need a receipt
Necesito un recibo (Ne-seh-_see_-toh oon reh-_see_-boh

AIRPORT
AEROPUERTO

arrival
llegadas (yeg-_ga_-dass)

departure
salidas (sa-_lee_-dass)

flight number
número de vuelo (_noo_-meh-roh deh _bweh_-loh)

delay
retraso (re-_tra_-soh)

check-in
facturación/chequeo de equipages (fak-too-ra-s'_yon_/cheh-_keh_-yoh deh ekkee-_pa_-khess)

hand luggage
equipaje de mano (ekkee-_pa_-khe deh _ma_-noh)

boarding card
tarjeta de embarque
(*tarr-kheh-ta deh
em-barr-keh*)

gate
puerta (*pwerr-ta*)

valid, invalid
válido, inválido (*ba-lee-
doh, eem-ba-lee-doh*)

**baggage/luggage
claim**
recolección de equipajes
(*rekko-lek-s'yon deh
ekkee-pa-khess*)

lost property office
oficina de objetos
perdidos (*offee-see-na
deh ob-khe-toss perr-
dee-doss*)

**Where do I get the
bus to the centre?**
¿Dónde tomo el autobús
a la ciudad?
(*Donn-deh toh-moh
ell aoo-toh-booss alla
see-oo-dad*)

**Where do I check in
for ...?**
¿Dónde está el mostrador
de ...? (*Donn-deh ess-ta
ell moss-tra-dorr deh ...*)

**An aisle/window
seat, please**
Un asiento en pasillo/
ventanilla, por favor
(*Oon ass-yen-toh en
pa-see-yoh/benta-nee-ya,
por fa-vor*)

**Where is the gate for
the flight to ....?**
¿Dónde está la puerta
de embarque para el
vuelo ...? (*Donn-deh
ess-ta la pwerr-ta deh
em-barr-keh parra ell
bweh-loh ...*)

**I have nothing to
declare**
Nada que declarar
(*Na-da keh dekla-rarr*)

**It's for my own
personal use**
Es de uso personal (*Ess
deh oo-soh perr-soh-nal*)

**The flight has been
cancelled**
El vuelo ha sido cancelado
(*Ell bweh-loh a see-doh
kan-seh-la-doh*)

**The flight has been
delayed**
El vuelo ha sido demorado
(*Ell bweh-loh a see-doh
demoh-ra-doh*)

ROAD TRAVEL/ CAR HIRE
VIAJE EN CARRETERA/ ALQUILER DE VEHÍCULOS

Have you got a road map?
¿Tiene un mapa carretero? (*T'yen-neh oon mappa karreh-teh-roh*)

How many kilometres is it to ...?
¿Cuántos kilómetros hay a ...? (*Kwan-toss kee-lommeh-tross aee a ...*)

Where is the nearest garage?
¿Dónde está el garaje más cercano? (*Donn-deh ess-ta ell ga-ra-kheh mahss ser-ka-noh*)

Fill it up, please
Llene el tanque, por favor (*Yen-neh ell tan-keh, por fa-vor*)

Please check the oil, water, battery, tyres
Por favor, controle el aceite, el agua, la batería, los neumáticos (*Por fa-vor, kon-troh-leh ell asay-teh, ell agwa, la ba-teh-ree-ya, loss neoo-ma-tee-koss*)

I'd like to hire a car
Quiero alquilar un coche (*K'yeh-roh al-kee-larr oon kotcheh*)

How much does it cost per day/week?
¿Cuánto cuesta por día/ semana? (*Kwan-toh kwess-ta porr dee-ya/ seh-ma-na*)

What do you charge per kilometre?
¿Cuánto cobran por kilómetro? (*Kwan-toh kob-ran porr kee-lommeh-troh*)

Is mileage unlimited?
¿El kilometraje es ilimitado? (*Ell keeloh-meh-tra-kheh ess ee-leemee-ta-doh*)

Where can I pick up the car?
¿Dónde recojo el coche? (*Donn-deh reh-koh-khoh ell kotcheh*)

Where can I leave the car?
¿Dónde puedo dejar el coche? (*Donn-deh pweh-doh deh-kharr ell kotcheh*)

garage
garaje/estación de servicio (ga-_ra_-kheh/ ess-ta-s'_yon_ deh serr-_vees_-yo)

headlights
luces, faros (_loo_-sess, _fa_-ross)

windscreen
parabrisas (parra-_bree_-sass)

indicator
intermitente, guiño, giro (een-termee-_ten_-teh, _geen_-yoh, _khee_-roh)

What is the speed limit?
¿Cuál es el límite de velocidad? (Kwal ess ell _lee_-mee-teh deh beh-loh-see-_dad_)

The keys are locked in the car
Las llaves están dentro del coche cerrado (Lass _ya_-vess ess-_tann_ _den_-troh dell _kot_cheh ser-_ra_-doh)

The engine is overheating
El motor está recalentado (Ell moh-_torr_ ess-_ta_ reh-kallen-_ta_-doh)

Have you got ...?
Tiene ...? (T'_yen_-neh ...)

- **a towing rope**
- una cuerda de remolque (oona _kwerr_-da deh reh-_moll_-keh)

- **a spanner**
- una llave de tuercas (oona _ya_-veh deh _twerr_-kass)

- **a screwdriver**
- un destornillador (oon dess-tornee-ya-_dorr_)

ROAD SIGNS
SEÑALES DE TRÁFICO

No through road
No pasar (Noh pas-_sarr_)

one-way street
calle de una sola mano (_ka_-yeh deh oona _solla_ _ma_-noh)

entrance
entrada (en-_tra_-da)

exit
salida (sa-_lee_-da)

danger
peligro (peh-_lee_-groh)

pedestrians
peatones
(peh-ya-toh-ness)

Keep entrance clear
No bloquear la entrada
*(Noh bloh-keh-yarr la
en-tra-da)*

Residents only
Sólo para residentes
*(Solloh parra reh-see-
den-tess)*

speed limit
límite de velocidad
*(lee-mee-teh deh
beh-loh-see-dad)*

stop
pare *(pa-reh)*

No entry
Prohibida la entrada *(Pro-
ee-bee-da la en-tra-da)*

roundabout
rotonda *(roh-ton-da)*

Insert coins
Ponga cambio/monedas
*(Pong-ga kam-b'yoh/
moh-neh-dass)*

No Parking
Prohibido estacionar
*(Pro-ee-bee-doh
es-ta-s'yoh-narr*

parking garage
garaje de estacionamiento
*(ga-ra-kheh deh ess-ta-
s'yon-na-m'yen-toh)*

supervised car park
estacionamiento
controlado *(ess-ta-s'yon-
na-m'yen-toh kon-troh-
la-doh)*

No right turn
Prohibido girar a la
derecha *(pro-ee-bee-doh
khee-rarr alla deh-retcha)*

cul de sac
calle sin salida *(ka-yeh
seen sa-lee-da)*

roadworks
trabajos camineros
*(tra-ba-khoss kamee-
neh-ross)*

detour
desvío *(dess-vee-oh)*

Caution
Cuidado *(Kwee-da-doh)*

uneven surface
calzada irregular *(kal-sa-da
ee-reh-goo-larr)*

toll
peaje *(peh-a-kheh)*

ACCOMMODATION
ALOJAMIENTO

bed & breakfast
pensión *(pen-s'yon)*

vacancies
habitación libre
*(abbee-ta-s'yon
lee-breh)*

Have you a room ...?
¿Tiene una habitación ...?
*(T'yenn-neh oona
abbee-ta-s'yon)*

♦ **for tonight**
♦ para esta noche
(parra ess-ta notcheh)

♦ **with breakfast**
♦ con desayuno *(kon
dessa-yoo-noh)*

♦ **with bath**
♦ con baño *(kon banyo)*

♦ **with shower**
♦ con ducha *(kon
dootcha)*

♦ **a single room**
♦ habitación single/para
una persona *(abbee-
ta-s'yon single/parra
oona per-soh-na)*

♦ **a double room**
♦ habitación doble
*(abbee-ta-s'yon
dob-bleh)*

♦ **a family room**
♦ habitación familiar
*(abbee-ta-s'yon
fa-meel-yar)*

**How much is the
room ...?**
¿Cuánto cuesta la
habitación ...?
*(Kwan-toh kwess-ta la
abbee-ta-s'yon)*

♦ **per day/week**
♦ por día/semana *(por
dee-ya/se-ma-na)*

**Have you got
anything better/
cheaper?**
¿Hay algo mejor/más
barato? *(Aee al-goh
meh-khorr/mahss
ba-ra-toh)*

May I see the room?
¿Puedo ver la
habitación? *(Pweh-doh
berr la abbee-ta-s'yon)*

Do you have a cot?
¿Tiene una cuna?
(T'yenn-neh oona koo-na)

What time is breakfast/dinner?
¿A qué hora es el desayuno/la cena? (A *keh oh-ra ess ell dessa-yoo-noh/la seh-na*)

room service
el servicio de cuarto/habitaciones (*ell serr-vee-s'yoh deh kwarr-toh/abbee-ta-s'yon-ness*)

Please bring ...
Por favor trae/traiga ... (*Por fa-vor tra-eh/traee-ga*)

♦ **toilet paper**
♦ papel higiénico (*pa-pell ee-khee-en-ee-koh*)

♦ **clean towels**
♦ toallas limpias (*toh-ay-yas leem-p'yass*)

Please clean the bath
Por favor limpia la bañera (*Por fa-vor leem-p'ya la ban-yeh-ra*)

Please put fresh sheets on the bed
Por favor, cambia las sábanas (*Por fa-vor, kam-b'ya lass sa-ba-nass*)

Please don't touch ...
Por favor, no toques ... (*Por fa-vor, noh tok-kess*)

♦ **my briefcase**
♦ mi maletín (*mee ma-leh-teen*)

♦ **my laptop**
♦ mi computador portátil (*mee kom-poo-ta-dorr porr-ta-teel*)

My ... doesn't work
Mi ... no funciona (*Mee ... noh foon-s'yoh-na*)

♦ **toilet**
♦ inodoro/lavabo (*eeno-doh-roh/la-va-boh*

♦ **bedside lamp**
♦ lámpara (*lam-pa-ra*)

♦ **air conditioning**
♦ aire acondicionado (*aee-reh akon-dee-s'yoh-na-doh*

There is no hot water
No hay agua caliente (*Noh aee agwa kallee-yen-teh*)

RECEPTION
RECEPCIÓN

Are there any messages for me?
¿Hay algún mensaje para mí? (*Aee al-goon men-sa-kheh parra mee*)

Has anyone asked for me?
¿Alguien ha preguntado por mí? (*Al-ghee-en a pre-goon-ta-doh porr mee*)

Can I leave a message for someone?
¿Puedo dejar un mensaje para alguien? (*Pweh-doh deh-khar oon men-sa-kheh parra al-ghee-en*)

Is there a laundry service?
¿Hay servicio de lavandería? (*Aee serr-vee-s'yoh de la-van-deh-ree-ya*)

I need a wake-up call at 7 o'clock
¿Puedes despertarme a las 7 en punto? (*Pweh-dess des-per-tarr-meh a lass s'yet-teh en poon-toh*)

What number must I dial for room service?
¿Cuál es el número de servicio de cuarto? (*Kwal ess ell noo-meh-roh deh serr-vee-s'yoh deh kwarr-toh*)

Where is the lift/elevator?
¿Dónde está el ascensor? (*Donn-deh ess-ta ell as-sen-sorr*)

Do you arrange tours?
¿Organiza los viajes? (*Orr-ga-nee-sa loss b'ya-khess*)

Please prepare the bill
Por favor, prepara la cuenta (*Por fa-vor, preh-parra la kwen-ta*)

There is a mistake in this bill
Hay un error en esta cuenta (*Aee oon error en ess-ta kwen-ta*)

I'm leaving tomorrow
Salgo mañana (*Sall-goh man-ya-na*)

SELF-CATERING
ALOJAMIENTO CON
COCINA PROPIA

**Have you any
vacancies?**
¿Hay lugar? (*Aee loo-garr*)

**How much is it
per night/week?**
¿Cuánto cuesta por
noche/semana?
(*Kwan-toh kwess-ta
porr notcheh*)

How big is it?
¿Cuál es el tamaño?
(*Kwal ess ell ta-man-yoh*)

**Do you allow
children?**
¿Se permiten niños? (*Seh
per-mee-ten neen-yoss*)

**Please, show me
how ... works**
Por favor, muéstrame
cómo funciona ...
(*Por fa-vor, mwess-tra-
meh kom-moh foon-
s'yoh-na ...*)

- **the cooker/stove/
  oven**
- la cocina/horno
  (*la koh-see-na/orr-noh*)

- **the washing
  machine**
- la lavadora
  (*la lava-doh-ra*)

- **the dryer**
- la secadora
  (*la se-ka-doh-ra*)

- **the hair-dryer**
- el secador de pelo
  (*ell se-ka-dorr deh
  peh-loh*)

- **the heater**
- el calefactor
  (*ell ka-leh-fak-torr*)

- **the water heater**
- el calentador para agua
  (*ell ka-lenta-dorr parra
  agwa*)

Where is/are ...?
¿Dónde está/están ...?
(*Donn-deh ess-ta/
ess-tan ...*)

- **the keys**
- las llaves (*lass ya-vess*)

- **the switch**
- el interruptor
  (*ell een-ter-roop-torr*)

- **the fuses**
- los fusibles
  (*loss foo-see-bless*)

Is there ...?
¿Hay ...? (*Aee ...*)

- **a cot**
- una cuna? (*oona koo-na*)

- **a high chair**
- una silla alta para niños
  (*oona see-ya alta parra neen-yoss*)

- **a safe**
- una caja fuerte (*oona ka-kha fwerr-teh*)

We need more ...
necesitamos más ... (*ne-seh-see-ta-moss mahss*)

- **cutlery**
- cubertería, cubiertos
  (*koo-ber-teh-ree-ya, koo-byerr-toss*)

- **crockery**
- vajilla (*ba-khee-ya*)

- **sheets**
- sábanas (*sa-ba-nass*)

- **blanket**
- frazada, cobija, manta
  (*fra-sa-da, koh-bee-kha, man-ta*)

- **pillows**
- almohadas
  (*al-moh-aa-dass*)

Is there ... in the vicinity?
¿Hay ... en el area?
(*Aee ... en ell a-reh-ya*)

- **a shop**
- una tienda, un negocio
  (*oona t'yen-da, oon neh-goh-s'yoh*)

- **a restaurant**
- un restaurante (*oon resta-oo-ran-teh*)

- **a bus/tram**
- un autobús/tranvía
  (*oon aoo-toh-booss/ tram-bee-ya*)

We'd like to stay for three nights/a week
Nos gustaría quedarnos por tres noches/una semana (*Nos goos-ta-ree-ya keh-darr-nos porr tress notchess/oona seh-ma-na*)

I have locked myself out
No puedo entrar (*No pweh-doh en-trar*)

The window won't open/close
La ventana no abre/cierra (*La ben-ta-na noh ab-reh/s'yer-ra*)

CAMPING
ACAMPAR

caravan
casa rodante/
autocaravana
(*ka-sa roh-dan-teh/*
aoo-toh-karra-va-na)

**Have you got a list
of campsites?**
¿Tiene una lista de sitios
para acampar? (*T'yen-neh*
oona lees-ta deh seet-
yoss parra a-kam-parr)

**Are there any sites
available?**
¿Hay sitios disponibles?
(*Aee seet-yoss*
dees-poh-nee-bless)

**How much is it
per night/week?**
¿Cuánto cuesta por
noche/semana?
(*Kwan-toh kwess-ta*
porr notcheh)

**Can we park the
caravan here?**
¿Podemos estacionar la
casa rodante aquí?
(*Poh-deh-moss es-ta-*
s'yoh-narr la ka-sa roh-
dan-teh a-kee)

**Can we camp here
overnight?**
¿Podemos acampar aquí
por la noche? (*Poh-deh-*
moss a-kam-parr a-kee
porr la notcheh)

**This site is very
muddy**
Este sitio está muy
enlodado/embarrado
(*Ess-te seet-yoh ess-ta*
moo-ee en-loh-da-doh/
em-bar-ra-doh)

**Is there a sheltered
site?**
¿Hay un sitio más
protegido? (*Aee oon*
seet-yo mahss
pro-teh-khee-doh)

**Do you have
electricity?**
¿Tienen electricidad?
(*T'yen-nen*
elek-tree-see-dad)

**Is there ... in the
vicinity?**
¿Hay ... en el area?
(*Aee ... en ell a-reh-ya*)

◆ **a shop**
◆ una tienda, un negocio
(*oona t'yen-da, oon*
neh-goh-s'yoh)

♦ **a restaurant**
♦ un restaurante *(oon resta-oo-ran-teh)*

♦ **an eating place**
♦ un lugar para comer *(oon loo-garr parra ko-merr)*

♦ **a garage**
♦ una estación de servicio *(oona es-ta-s'yon deh serr-vee-s'yoh)*

We'd like to stay for three nights/a week
Nos gustaría quedarnos por tres noches/una semana *(Nos goos-ta-ree-ya keh-darr-nos porr tress notchess/oona seh-ma-na)*

Is there drinking water?
¿Hay agua potable? *(Aee agwa poh-ta-bleh)*

Can I light a fire here?
¿Puedo encender fuego aquí? *(Pweh-doh en-sen-derr fweh-goh a-kee)*

I'd like to buy fire wood
Me gustaría comprar leña *(Meh goos-ta-ree-a kom-prarr lehn-ya)*

Is the wood dry?
¿Está seca la leña? *(Ess-ta seh-ka la lehn-ya)*

Do you have ... for rent?
¿Tienen ... para alquilar? *(T'yen-nen ... parra al-kee-larr)*

♦ **a tent**
♦ una tienda *(oona t'yen-da)*

♦ **a gas cylinder**
♦ una bombona *(oona bom-boh-na)*

♦ **a groundsheet**
♦ un aislante para el suelo *(oon aees-lan-teh parra ell sweh-loh)*

Where is/are the nearest ...?
¿Dónde está/están ... más cercano? *(Donn-deh ess-ta/ess-tan ... mahss serr-ka-noh)*

♦ **toilets**
♦ los baños *(loss ban-yoss)*

♦ **sink (for dishes)**
♦ lavadero *(la-va-deh-roh)*

CUTLERY
CUBERTERÍA

knife
cuchillo *(koo-chee-yoh)*

fork, cake fork
tenedor, tenedor de torta *(ten-eh-dorr, ten-eh-dorr deh torr-ta)*

spoon, teaspoon
cuchara, cucharita *(koo-cha-ra, koo-cha-ree-ta)*

crockery
vajilla *(ba-khee-ya)*

plate
plato *(pla-toh)*

cup and saucer, mug
pocillo y platillo, taza *(poh-see-yo ee pla-tee-yo, ta-sa)*

BREAKFAST
DESAYUNO

coffee
café *(ka-feh)*

◆ **black**
◆ solo *(solloh)*

◆ **with milk, cream**
◆ con leche, crema *(kon letcheh, kreh-ma)*

◆ **without sugar**
◆ sin azúcar *(seen a-soo-karr)*

tea
té *(teh)*

◆ **with milk, lemon**
◆ con leche, limón *(kon letcheh, lee-mon)*

bread
pan *(pan)*

rolls
panecillos *(pa-neh-see-yoss)*

egg(s)
huevo(s) *(ooweh-voss)*

◆ **boiled – soft, hard**
◆ pasados por agua – ligeros, duros *(pas-sa-doss porr agwa – lee-khe-ross, doo-ross)*

◆ **fried**
◆ fritos *(free-toss)*

◆ **scrambled**
◆ revueltos *(rev-wel-toss)*

◆ poached
◆ escalfados
(es-kal-**fa**-doss)

◆ bacon and eggs
◆ tocino y huevos
(toh-**see**-noh ee
oo**weh**-voss)

cereal
cereal (seh-reh-**al**)

hot milk, cold milk
leche caliente, leche fría
(**let**cheh kall-**yen**-teh,
letcheh **free**-ya)

fruit
fruta (**froo**-ta)

orange juice
zumo/jugo de naranja
(**soo**-moh/**khoo**-goh deh
na-**ran**-kha)

jam
jalea/mermelada
(kha-**leh**-a/mer-meh-**la**-da)

marmalade
mermelada
(mer-meh-**la**-da)

pepper
pimienta (peem-**yen**-ta)

salt
sal (**sal**)

LUNCH/DINNER
ALMUERZO/
COMIDA/CENA

Could we have a table ...?
¿Tiene una mesa ...?
(T'**yen**-neh oona **meh**-sa)

◆ by the window
◆ junto a la ventana
(**khoon**-toh alla
ben-**ta**-na)

◆ outside
◆ fuera (**fweh**-ra)

◆ inside
◆ dentro (**den**-troh)

May I have ... ?
¿Puedo ordenar ... ?
(**Pweh**-doh or-deh-**narr**)

◆ the wine list
◆ la carta de vinos (la
karr-ta deh **bee**-noss)

◆ the menu of the day
◆ el menú del día (ell
meh-**noo** dell **dee**-ya)

◆ starters
◆ entrada
(en-**tra**-da)

◆ **main course**
◆ plato principal
(_pla_-toh preen-see-_pal_)

◆ **dessert**
◆ postre (_poss_-treh)

◆ **the menu**
◆ el menú
(ell meh-_noo_)

I'll take the set menu
Comeré el menú fijo
(Ko-meh-_reh_ ell meh-_noo_
fee-khoh)

What is this?
¿Qué es ésto?
(_Keh_ ess _ess_-toh)

**That is not what I
ordered**
Esto no es lo que he
ordenado (_Ess_-toh
noh ess loh keh eh
orr-deh-_na_-doh)

It's tough, cold, off
Está duro, frío, podrido
(Ess-_ta_ _doo_-roh,
free-yoh, pod-_ree_-doh)

**What do you
recommend?**
¿Qué me recomienda?
(Keh meh rekko-
m'_yen_-da)

**Can I have the bill
please?**
¿Me trae la cuenta, por
favor? (Meh _tra_-eh la
kwen-ta, por fa-_vor_)

**We'd like to pay
separately**
Queremos pagar en
forma separada
(Keh-_reh_-moss pa-_garr_
en _for_-ma seppa-_ra_-da)

There is a mistake
Hay un error
(_Aee_ oon er_ror_)

**Thank you, that's
for you**
Gracias, esto es para
usted (_Graas_-yass, _ess_-
toh ess parra oos-_ted_)

Keep the change
Quédese con el cambio
(_Keh_-deh-seh kon ell
kam-b'yoh)

DRINKS
BEBIDAS

**a beer/lager – large,
small**
una cerveza – grande,
pequeña (oona
serr-_veh_-sa – _grann_-deh,
peh-_kehn_-ya

glass (¼ litre) of cider
un vaso (un cuarto) de
sidra (oon _ba_-soh [oon
kwarr-toh] deh _seed_-ra)

a dry white wine
un vino blanco seco
(oon _bee_-noh _blan_-koh
sek-koh)

a sweet white wine
un vino dulce
(oon _bee_-noh _dool_-seh)

a light red wine
un vino tinto liviano
(oon _bee_-noh _teen_-toh
lee-b_yah_-noh)

**a full-bodied red
wine**
un vino tinto con cuerpo
(oon _bee_-noh _teen_-toh
kon _kwerr_-poh)

new wine
vino nuevo (_bee_-noh
nweh-voh)

house wine
vino de la casa (_bee_-noh
della _ka_-sa)

**a glass of wine with
soda water**
un vaso de vino con soda
(oon _ba_-soh deh
bee-noh kon _soh_-da)

punch
ponche (_ponn_-cheh)

champagne
espumante, champaña
(es-poo-_man_-teh,
cham-_pann_-yah)

a brandy
un brandy (oon brandy)

a whisky with ice
un whisky con hielo
(oon whisky kon
yeh-loh)

liqueur
licor (lee-_korr_)

a glass
una copa
(oona _kop_-pa)

a bottle
una botella
(oona boh-_tey_-ya)

**a mineral water –
still, sparkling**
agua mineral – sin gas,
con gas
(_agwa_ mee-neh-_rall_ –
seen gass, _kon_ gass)

tap water
agua del grifo
(_agwa_ dell _gree_-foh)

fruit juice
zumo/jugo de fruta
(_soo_-moh/_khoo_-goh
deh _froo_-ta)

cola and lemonade
cola y limonada (_koh_-la
ee lee-moh-_na_-da)

another ... please
otro ... por favor (_otroh_ ...
por fa-_vor_)

too cold
demasiado frío (deh-
mass-_ya_-doh _free_-yoh)

not cold enough
no está suficientemente
frío (_noh_ ess-_ta_
soo-fee-s'_yen_-teh-
menteh _free_-yoh)

FOOD
COMIDA

Soup, Cream Soup
Sopa, Sopa Crema
(_soh_-pa, _soh_-pa _kreh_-ma)

**potato soup, mush-
room soup**
sopa de papa, sopa de
champiñones (_soh_-pa
deh _pappa_, _soh_-pa deh
cham-peen-_yoh_-ness)

cabbage soup
sopa de repollo (_soh_-pa
deh reh-_poy_-yoh

pea soup, bean soup
sopa de arvejas, sopa de
frijoles (_soh_-pa deh ar-
beh-khass, _soh_-pa deh
free-_khoh_-less)

consommé
consomé (kon-som-_meh_)

Fish
Pescado (pess-_ka_-doh)

sole
lenguado (leng-_gwa_-doh)

cod
bacalao (ba-ka-_laoo_)

perch
perca (_perr_-ca)

salmon
salmón (sal-_mon_)

herring
arenque (a-_reng_-keh)

trout
trucha (_troo_-cha)

tuna
atún (a-_toon_)

fried, grilled, sautéed
frito, a la parrilla, salteado
(*free-toh, alla pa-reey-ya, sal-teh-ya-doh*)

POULTRY
AVES (*a-vess*)

chicken
pollo (*poy-yoh*)

crumbed roasted chicken
suprema de pollo
(*soo-preh-ma deh poy-yoh*)

duck
pato (*pa-toh*)

goose
ganso (*gann-soh*)

roasted
asado (*a-sa-doh*)

MEAT
CARNE (*karr-neh*)

veal
carne de ternera
(*karr-neh deh terr-neh-ra*)

mutton, lamb
carne de cordero
(*karr-neh deh kor-deh-roh*)

beef
carne de vaca (*karr-neh deh ba-ka*)

pork
carne de cerdo (*karr-neh deh serr-doh*)

sausage
salchicha (*sal-chee-cha*)

veal sausage
salchicha de ternera (*sal-chee-cha deh terr-neh-ra*)

venison
venado (*be-na-doh*)

crumbed escalopes
escalopas apanadas
(*es-ka-loh-pass a-pa-na-dass*)

meat balls/cakes
bolas de carne
(*boh-las deh karr-neh*)

well done, medium, rare
bien hecho, medio hecho, poco hecho (*b'yen etchoh, med-yo etchoh, poh-koh etchoh*)

boiled, stewed
hervido, en compota (*err-bee-doh, en kom-poh-ta*)

smoked meats
fiambres ahumados
(f'*yam*-bress aoo-*ma*-doss)

platter of cold meats
un plato de fiambres (oon *pla*-toh deh f'*yam*-bress)

PASTA AND RICE
PASTA Y ARROZ
(*pas*-ta ee ar-*ross*)

pasta made with cottage cheese
pasta hecha con queso untable (*pas*-ta *etcha* kon *keh*-soh oon-*ta*-bleh)

pasta with tomato sauce
pasta con salsa de tomate (*pas*-ta kon *sal*-sa deh toh-*ma*-teh)

rice
arroz (ar-*ross*)

VEGETABLES, SALAD AND FRUIT
VERDURAS, ENSALADA Y FRUTA (ber-*doo*-rass, en-sa-*la*-da ee *froo*-ta)

eggplant
berenjena
(beh-ren-*khe*-na)

onion
cebolla (seh-*boy*-ya)

cabbage
repollo (reh-*poy*-yoh)

cauliflower
coliflor (kollee-*florr*)

carrots
zanahorias
(sana-*oh*-r'yas)

green beans
habichuelas
(abbee-*chwe*-lass)

leeks
puerros (*pwer*-ross)

asparagus
espárragos
(es-*parra*-goss)

peppers
pimiento (peem-*yen*-toh)

pumpkin
zapallo, calabaza
(sa-*pay*-yoh, kalla-*ba*-sa)

potatoes – boiled, fried, mashed
papas – hervidas, fritas, puré de papas
(*pappass* – err-*bee*-dass, *free*-tass, poo-*reh* deh *pappass*)

lettuce
lechuga (leh-_choo_-ga)

beetroot
remolacha, betarraga
(remmo-_la_-cha,
bet-tar-_ra_-ga)

cucumber
pepino (peh-_pee_-noh)

root celery
apio (_ap_-yoh)

lemon
limón (lee-_mon_)

grapefruit
pomelo (poh-_meh_-loh)

apples
manzanas (man-_sa_-nass)

pears
peras (_peh_-rass)

bananas
plátanos/bananas
(_pla_-ta-noss, ba-_na_-nass)

pineapple
piñas/ananás
(_peen_-yass, a-na-_nass_)

raspberries
frambuesas
(fram-_bweh_-sass)

cherries
cerezas (seh-_reh_-sass)

strawberries
frutillas (froo-_tee_-yass)

apricots
damascos (da-_mass_-koss)

peaches
duraznos (doo-_ras_-noss)

blackberries
moras (_moh_-rass)

plums
ciruelas (seer-_weh_-lass)

prunes
ciruelas pasas
(seer-_weh_-lass _pas_-sas)

grapes
uvas (_oo_-vass)

dried fruit
fruta seca/disecada
(_froo_-ta _seh_-ka/
dee-seh-_ka_-da)

**passion fruit,
grenadilla**
maracuyá (ma-ra-coo-_ya_)

cranberries
arándanos (a-_ran_-da-noss)

DESSERTS AND CAKES
POSTRES Y PASTELES

fruit salad
ensalada de frutas (*en-sa-la-da deh froo-tass*)

jelly
gelatina (*khe-la-tee-na*)

crème caramel
flan (*flan*)

meringue
merengue (*meh-reng-geh*)

pastry with apples and raisins
tarta de manzanas (*tarr-ta deh man-sa-nass*)

light fruitcake
tarta de frutas (*tarr-ta deh froo-tass*)

plain sponge with crumble topping
bizcocho (*bees-kotchoh*)

fruit flan
flan de frutas (*flan deh froo-tass*)

marble cake
torta marmolada (*torr-ta marr-moh-la-da*)

cheesecake
pastel de queso (*pass-tell deh keh-soh*)

gateau with cherries and cream
torta con cerezas y crema (*torr-ta con seh-reh-sass ee kreh-ma*)

poppyseed cake
torta con semillas de amapola (*torr-ta con seh-mee-yass deh amma-poh-la*)

honey and almond tart
tarta de miel y almendras (*tarr-ta deh myell ee al-men-drass*)

sponge cake with chocolate
bizcochuelo con chocolate (*bee-scot-chweh-lo con chokkoh-la-teh*)

crème caramel with raspberry jam
flan con jalea de frambuesa (*flan con kha-leh-ya deh fram-bweh-sa*)

gingerbread biscuits
galletitas de jengibre (*ga-yeh-tee-tass deh khen-khee-breh*)

MONEY
DINERO

bureau de change
cambio/agencia de cambio *(kam-b'yoh/ a-khen-s'ya deh kam-b'yoh)*

cash dispenser/ATM
cajero automático *(ka-kheh-roh aoo-toh-ma-tee-koh)*

Where can I change money?
¿Dónde puedo cambiar dinero? *(Donn-deh pweh-doh kam-b'yarr dee-neh-roh)*

Where is an ATM, a bank?
¿Dónde hay un cajero automático, un banco? *(Donn-deh aee oon ka-kheh-roh aoo-toh-ma-tee-koh, oon bang-koh)*

When does the bank open/close?
¿A qué hora abre/cierra el banco? *(A keh oh-ra a-breh/s'yer-ra ell bang-koh)*

How much commission do you charge?
¿Cuánta comisión cobran? *(Kwan-ta ko-mee-s'yon kob-ran)*

I want to ...
Quiero ... *(Kyeh-roh ...)*

◆ **cash a traveller's cheque**
◆ cambiar cheques de viajero *(kam-b'yarr cheh-kess deh bee-a-kheh-roh)*

◆ **change £50**
◆ cambiar cincuenta libras *(kam-b'yarr seeng-kwen-ta lee-brass)*

◆ **make a transfer**
◆ hacer una transferencia *(a-serr oona trans-feh-ren-s'ya)*

POST OFFICE
OFICINA DE CORREOS

How much is ...?
¿Cuánto cuesta ...? *(Kwan-toh kwess-ta)*

◆ **a letter**
◆ una carta *(oona karr-ta)*

◆ **a postcard to ...**
◆ una postal a ...
  (oona poss-tal a ...)

◆ **a small parcel**
◆ un paquete pequeño
  *(oon pa-keh-teh
  peh-kehn-yoh)*

**Where can I buy
stamps?**
¿Dónde puedo comprar
estampillas? *(Donn-deh
pweh-doh kom-prarr
es-tam-peey-yass)*

SHOPPING
COMPRAS

What does it cost?
¿Cuánto cuesta? *(Kwan-
toh kwess-ta)*

How much is it (total)?
¿Cuánto es todo? *(Kwan-toh ess toddoh)*

I need a receipt
Necesito un recibo
*(ne-seh-see-toh oon
reh-see-boh)*

**Do you accept credit
cards?**
¿Se aceptan tarjetas de
crédito? *(Seh a-sep-tan
tarr-kheh-tass deh
kreh-dee-toh)*

**Do you take
traveller's cheques?**
¿Se aceptan cheques de
viajero? *(Seh a-sep-tan
cheh-kess deh
bee-a-kheh-roh)*

Where do I pay?
¿Dónde pago?
(Donn-deh pa-goh)

**Does that include
VAT?**
¿El IVA está incluido?
*(Ell ee oo-veh a ess-ta
een-kloo-ee-doh)*

**Do you need a
deposit?**
¿Necesita un depósito?
*(ne-seh-see-ta oon
deh-poh-see-toh)*

**Can you wrap it up
for me?**
¿Puedes envolverlo?
*(Pweh-dess
em-bol-verr-loh)*

This isn't what I want
Esto no es lo que yo
quiero *(Ess-toh noh ess
loh keh yoh k'yeh-roh)*

This isn't correct (bill)
Esto no es correcto (la
cuenta)*(Ess-toh noh ess
koh-rek-toh)*

I want my money back
Quiero de vuelta mi dinero (K'_yeh_-roh deh _bwell_-ta mee dee-_neh_-roh)

This is ...
Esto está ... (_Ess_-toh ess-_ta_ ...)

◆ **broken**
◆ roto (_roh_-toh)

◆ **damaged**
◆ dañado (dan-_ya_-doh

Can you repair it?
¿Puede repararlo? (_Pweh_-deh reppa-_rarr_-loh)

BUYING FOOD
COMPRA DE COMIDA

Where can I buy ...?
¿Dónde puedo comprar ...? (_Donn_-deh _pweh_-doh kom-_prarr_)

◆ **bread**
◆ pan (_pan_)

◆ **cake**
◆ pastel/torta (pass-_tell_/ _torr_-ta)

◆ **cheese**
◆ queso (_keh_-soh)

◆ **butter**
◆ mantequilla (man-teh-_kee_-ya)

◆ **milk**
◆ leche (_letcheh_)

◆ **water**
◆ agua (_agwa_)

◆ **wine**
◆ vino (_bee_-noh)

◆ **sparkling wine**
◆ vino espumante (_bee_-noh es-poo-_man_-teh)

◆ **beer**
◆ cerveza (serr-_veh_-sa)

◆ **fruit juice**
◆ jugo/zumo de fruta (_khoo_-goh/_soo_-moh deh _froo_-ta)

◆ **meat**
◆ carne (_karr_-neh)

◆ **ham**
◆ jamón (kha-_monn_)

◆ **polony/cold meats**
◆ fiambres (_fyam_-bress)

◆ **vegetables**
◆ verduras (ber-_doo_-rass)

- **fruit**
- fruta (*froo-ta*)

- **eggs**
- huevos (*ooweh-voss*)

I'll take ...
Llevo ... (*Yeh-voh ...*)

- **one kilo**
- un kilo (*oon kee-loh*)

- **three slices**
- tres rebanadas (*tress rebba-na-dass*)

- **a portion of**
- una porción de (*oona por-s'yon deh*)

- **a packet of**
- un paquete de (*oon pa-keh-teh deh*)

- **a dozen**
- una docena (*oona doh-seh-na*)

BUYING CLOTHES
COMPRA DE ROPA

Can I try this on?
¿Puedo probarlo? (*Pweh-doh proh-barr-loh*)

It is ...
Es ... (*Ess ...*)

- **too big**
- demasiado grande (*deh-mass-ya-doh grann-deh*)

- **too small**
- demasiado pequeño (*deh-mass-ya-doh peh-kehn-yoh*)

- **too tight**
- demasiado ajustado (*deh-mass-ya-doh a-khoos-ta-doh*)

- **too wide**
- demasiado ancho (*deh-mass-ya-doh anchoh*)

- **too expensive**
- demasiado caro (*deh-mass-ya-doh ka-roh*)

I'll take ...
Llevo ... (*Yeh-voh ...*)

- **this one**
- éste/ésta (*ess-teh/ess-ta*)

- **size 40**
- talla/talle 40 (*tay-ya/tay-yeh kwa-ren-ta*)

- **two**
- dos (*doss*)

CLOTHING SIZES – TALLAS DE ROPA

Women's Wear

UK	Cont. Europe	USA
10	38	8
12	40	10
14	42	12
16	44	14
18	46	16

Menswear

UK	Cont. Europe	USA
36	46	36
38	48	38
40	50	40
42	52	42
44	54	44
46	56	46

Men's Shirts

UK	Cont. Europe	USA
14	36	14
14.5	37	14.5
15	38	15
15.5	39	15.5
16	41	16
17	43	17

Shoes

UK	Cont. Europe	USA
5	39	6
6	40	7
7	41	8
8	42	9
9	43	10
10	44	11
11	45	12

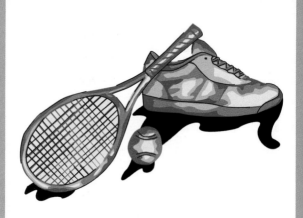

SIGHTSEEING
TURISMO

tourist office
oficina de turismo *(offee-see-na deh too-rees-moh)*

Do you have brochures/leaflets?
¿Tiene folletos? *(T'yen-neh foy-yeh-toss)*

I/We want to visit ...
Queremos visitar ... *(Kehr-reh-moss bee-see-tarr ...)*

When is it open/closed?
¿A qué hora abre/cierra? *(A keh oh-ra ab-reh/s'yer-ra)*

What does it cost?
¿Cuánto cuesta? *(Kwan-toh kwess-ta)*

Are there any reductions for ...?
¿Hay descuento para ...? *(Aee des-kwen-toh parra)*

◆ **children**
◆ niños *(neen-yoss)*

◆ **senior citizens**
◆ jubilados *(khoo-bee-la-doss)*

◆ **students**
◆ estudiantes *(es-toodee-yan-tess)*

Are there any tours?
¿Hay visitas guiadas? *(Aee bee-see-tass gee-ya-dass)*

When does the bus depart/return?
¿Cuándo sale/regresa el autobús? *(Kwan-doh sa-leh/reh-gres-sa ell aoo-toh-booss)*

From where does the bus leave?
¿De dónde sale el autobús? *(Deh donn-deh sa-leh ell aoo-toh-booss)*

Where is the museum?
¿Dónde está el museo? *(Donn-deh ess-ta ell moo-seh-yoh)*

How much is the entrance fee?
¿Cuánto cuesta la entrada? *(Kwan-toh kwess-ta la en-tra-da)*

ENTERTAINMENT
DIVERSIÓN

Is there a list of cultural events?
¿Hay una lista/guía de eventos culturales?
(_Aee_ oona _lees_-ta/_gee_-ya deh eh-_ven_-toss kool-too-_ra_-less)

Are there any festivals?
¿Hay algún festival?
(_Aee_ al-_goon_ fes-tee-_val_)

I'd like to go to ...
Quiero ir ... (K'_yeh_-roh eer ...)

◆ the theatre
◆ al teatro (al teh-_a_-tro)

◆ the opera
◆ a la ópera
(alla _oh_-peh-ra)

◆ the ballet
◆ al ballet (al ba-_yeh_)

◆ the cinema/movies
◆ al cine (al _see_-neh)

◆ a concert
◆ a un concierto
(a oon kon-s'_yer_-toh)

Do I have to book?
¿Debo reservar?
(_Debboh_ reh-ser-_varr_)

How much are the tickets?
¿Cuánto cuestan los billetes? (_Kwan_-toh _kwess_-tan loss bee-_yet_-tess)

Two tickets for ...
Dos billetes para ... (_Doss_ bee-_yet_-tess parra)

◆ tonight
◆ esta noche (_ess_-ta _not_cheh)

◆ tomorrow night
◆ mañana por la noche (man-_ya_-na porr la _not_cheh)

◆ the early show
◆ la matiné (la ma-tee-_neh_)

◆ the late show
◆ el espectáculo más tarde (ell es-pek-_ta_-coo-loh _mahss_ _tarr_-deh)

When does the performance start/end?
¿A qué hora comienza/termina la función? (A keh _oh_-ra koh-m'_yen_-sa/_terr_-mee-na la foon-s'_yon_)

Where is ...?
¿Dónde hay ...?
(Donn-deh aee ...)

- **a good bar**
- un buen bar *(oon bwen barr)*

- **good live music**
- buena música en vivo *(bweh-na moo-see-ka en bee-voh)*

Is it ...?
Es/Está ...? *(Ess/Ess-ta ...)*

- **expensive**
- caro *(ka-roh)*

- **noisy, crowded**
- ruidoso, muy lleno *(rooee-doh-soh, mooee yen-noh)*

How do I get there?
¿Cómo llego allí? *(kom-moh yeh-goh a-yee)*

SPORT
DEPORTES

Where can we ...?
¿Dónde podemos ...? *(Donn-deh poh-deh-moss)*

- **go skiing**
- esquiar *(es-kee-yarr)*

- **play tennis/golf**
- jugar al tenis/golf *(khoo-garr al ten-nees/golf)*

- **go swimming**
- nadar *(na-darr)*

- **go fishing**
- pescar *(pess-karr)*

- **go riding**
- cabalgar *(ka-bal-garr)*

- **go cycling**
- andar/montar en bicicleta *(an-darr/mon-tarr en bee-see-kleh-ta)*

- **hire bicycles**
- alquilar bicicletas *(al-kee-larr bee-see-kleh-tass)*

- **hire tackle**
- alquilar equipos de pesca *(al-kee-larr eh-kee-poss deh pess-ka)*

- **hire golf clubs**
- alquilar palos de golf *(al-kee-larr pa-loss deh golf)*

- **hire skis**
- alquilar esquís *(al-kee-larr es-keess)*

- **hire a boat**
- alquilar un barco/un bote/una lancha *(al-kee-larr oon barr-koh/ oon boh-teh/ oona lan-cha)*

- **hire skates**
- alquilar patines *(al-kee-larr pa-tee-ness)*

- **hire an umbrella**
- alquilar una sombrilla *(al-kee-larr oona som-bree-ya)*

- **hire a deck chair**
- alquilar una silla para el sol *(al-kee-larr oona see-ya parra ell sol)*

How much is it ...?
¿Cuánto cuesta ...? *(Kwan-toh kwess-ta ...)*

- **per hour**
- por hora *(porr oh-ra)*

- **per day**
- por día *(porr dee-ya)*

- **per session/game**
- por sesión/juego *(porr sess-yon/khweh-goh)*

Is it ...?
Es ...? *(Ess ...)*

- **deep**
- profundo *(proh-foon-doh)*

- **clean**
- limpio *(leem-pyoh)*

- **cold**
- frío *(free-yoh)*

How do we get there?
¿Cómo llegamos allí? *(Koh-moh yeh-ga-moss a-yee)*

No swimming/diving
Prohibido nadar/zambullirse *(Pro-ee-bee-doh na-darr/sam-boo-yeer-seh)*

Are there currents?
¿Hay corrientes? *(Aee korr-yen-tess)*

Do I need a fishing permit?
¿Necesito un permiso de pesca? *(Ne-seh-see-toh oon per-mee-soh deh pess-ka)*

Where can I get one?
¿Dónde puedo obtenerlo? *(Donn-deh pweh-doh ob-teh-nerr-lo)*

Is there a guide for walks?
¿Hay un guía para las caminatas? (*Aee oon gee*-ya parra lass kamee-*na*-tass)

Do I need walking boots?
¿Necesito botas para la caminata? (neh-seh-*see*-toh *boh*-tass parra lah kamee-*na*-ta)

How much is a ski pass?
¿Cuánto cuesta un pase de esquí? (*Kwan*-toh *kwess*-ta oon pa-seh deh es-*kee*)

Is it safe to ski today?
¿Es seguro esquiar hoy? (Ess seh-*goo*-roh es-kee-*yarr* oy)

Run closed
Pista cerrada (*Pees*-ta ser-*ra*-da)

avalanches
avalanchas (ava-*lan*-chass)

I'm a beginner
Soy principiante (*Soy* preen-see-pee-*an*-teh)

Danger
Peligro (peh-*lee*-groh)

Which is an easy run?
¿Cuál es una pista fácil? (*Kwal* ess oona *pees*-ta *fa*-seel)

My skis are too long/short
Mis esquís son demasiado largos/cortos (Mees es-*keess* sonn de-mass-*ya*-doh *larr*-goss/*korr*-toss)

We want to go ...
Queremos ir ... (Keh-*reh*-moss eer ...)

- ◆ **hiking**
- ◆ de caminata (deh kamee-*na*-ta)

- ◆ **sailing**
- ◆ a navegar (a na-veh-*garr*)

- ◆ **ice-skating**
- ◆ a patinar sobre hielo (a pa-tee-*narr* sob-breh *yeh*-loh)

- ◆ **water-skiing**
- ◆ a hacer esquí acuático (a a-*serr* es-*kee* akoo-*a*-tee-koh)

PHARMACY/ CHEMIST
FARMACIA

health shop
tienda de medicinas naturales (*t'yen-da deh meddee-see-nass na-too-ra-less*)

Have you got something for ...?
¿Tiene algo para ...? (*T'yn-neh al-goh parra ...*)

♦ **diarrhoea**
♦ diarrea (*dee-ya-reh-ya*)

♦ **cold, flu**
♦ resfriado, gripe (*ress-free-a-doh, gree-peh*)

♦ **headache**
♦ dolor de cabeza (*doh-lorr de ka-beh-sa*)

♦ **a sore throat**
♦ dolor de garganta (*doh-lorr de garr-gan-ta*)

♦ **stomachache**
♦ dolor de estómago (*doh-lorr de es-toh-ma-goh*)

♦ **car sickness**
♦ mareo de viaje en coche (*ma-reh-yoh deh bee-a-kheh en kotcheh*)

I need ...
Necesito ... (*Ne-seh-see-toh ...*)

♦ **indigestion tablets**
♦ tabletas para indigestión (*tab-leh-tass parra een-dee-khess-t'yon*)

♦ **laxative**
♦ laxativo (*lax-a-tee-voh*)

♦ **sleeping tablets**
♦ tabletas para dormir (*tab-leh-tass parra dorr-meer*)

♦ **a painkiller**
♦ un analgésico (*oon annal-kheh-see-koh*)

Is it safe for children?
¿Es seguro para niños? (*Ess seh-goo-roh parra neen-yoss*)

I'm a diabetic
Soy diabético (*Soy dee-ya-bet-tee-koh*)

I have high blood pressure
Sufro de presión alta
(_Soo_-froh deh
pres-see-_on_ _alta_)

I'm allergic to ...
Soy alérgico a ... (_Soy_
a-_lerr_-khee-koh a ...)

I have toothache
Me duelen los dientes
(_Meh_ _dweh_-len loss
dee-_en_-tess)

optometrist
optometrista
(op-toh-meh-_trees_-ta)

DOCTOR
MÉDICO

I am ill
Estoy enfermo
(_Estoy_ en-_ferr_-moh)

I need a doctor
Necesito un médico
(Ne-seh-_see_-toh oon
med-dee-koh)

He/she has a high temperature
Tiene fiebre
(T'_yen_-neh fee-_eb_-reh)

It hurts
Duele (_Dweh_-leh)

I am going to be sick!
¡Voy a vomitar!
(_Boy_ a bo-mee-_tarr_)

dentist
dentista (den-_tees_-ta)

HOSPITAL
HOSPITAL

Will I have to go to hospital?
¿Debo ir al
hospital? (_Debboh_ eer
al oss-pee-_tal_)

Where is the hospital?
¿Dónde está el hospital?
(_Donn_-deh ess-_ta_
ell oss-pee-_tal_)

Which ward?
¿Cuál sala? (_Kwal_ _sa_-la)

When are visiting hours?
¿Cuál es el horario de
visita? (_Kwal_ ess ell oh-
raar-yoh deh _bee_-see-ta)

Where is casualty?
¿Dónde están las urgen-
cias? (_Donn_-deh ess-_tan_
lass oor-khens-yass)

POLICE
POLICÍA

Call the police
Llame a la policía *(Ya-meh alla pollee-see-ya)*

I have been robbed
Me han robado
(Meh an ro-ba-doh)

My car has been stolen
Han robado mi coche *(An ro-ba-doh mee kotcheh)*

My car has been broken into
Han robado de mi coche *(An ro-ba-doh deh mee kotcheh)*

I want to report a theft
Quiero denunciar un robo *(K'yeh-roh deh-noon-see-yarr oon roh-boh)*

I have been attacked
Me han atacado
(Meh an atta-ka-doh)

I have been raped
Me han violado
(Meh an bee-oh-la-doh)

Where is the police station?
¿Dónde está la oficina de policía/comisaría? *(Donn-deh ess-ta la offee-see-na deh pollee-see-ya)*

EMERGENCIES
EMERGENCIAS

Call an ambulance
Llame una ambulancia *(Ya-meh oona amboo-lan-s'ya)*

There's been an accident
Hubo un accidente *(Oo-boh oon ak-see-den-teh)*

Someone is injured
Alguien está herido *(Al-gee-yen ess-ta eh-ree-doh)*

Hurry up!
¡Date prisa!
(Da-teh pree-sa)

Could you please help me?
¿Puede ayudarme por favor? *(Pweh-deh a-yoo-darr-meh por fa-vor)*

Help!
¡Ayúdeme!
(a-_yoo_-deh-meh)

This is an emergency!
¡Esto es una emergencia!
(_Ess_-toh ess oona
em-merr-_khen_-s'ya)

My son/daughter is missing
Mi hijo/hija está desa-
parecido/a, perdido/a
(Mee _ee_-khoh/_ee_-kha
ess-_ta_ dessa-parreh-
see-doh/da, perr-_dee_-
doh/da)

I need a report for my insurance
Necesito un informe para
mi seguro (Ne-seh-_see_-
toh oon een-_forr_-meh
parra mee seh-_goo_-roh)

I want to phone my embassy
Quiero llamar a mi
embajada (K'_yeh_-roh _ya_-
marr mee em-ba-_kha_-da)

I am lost
Estoy perdido
(_Estoy_ per-_dee_-doh)

He/she is ill
Está enfermo/a
(Ess-_ta_ en-_ferr_-moh/ma)

FIRE DEPARTMENT
BOMBEROS

Fire!
¡Fuego! (_Fweh_-goh)

Look out!
¡Cuídese! (_Kee_-deh-seh)

Call the fire department
Llame a los bomberos
(_Ya_-meh a loss
bom-_beh_-ross)

It's an electrical fire
Es un incendio eléctrico
(Ess oon een-_senn_-d'yoh
elek-tree-koh)

The address is ...
La dirección es ... (La
dee-rek-s'_yon_ ess ...)

I need ...
Necesito ...
(Ne-seh-_see_-toh ...)

◆ **a fire extinguisher**
◆ un extinguidor
   (oon ex-ting-_ghee_-
   dorr)

◆ **medical assistance**
◆ ayuda médica
   (a-_yoo_-da _meh_-dee-ka)

THE HUMAN BODY
EL CUERPO HUMANO

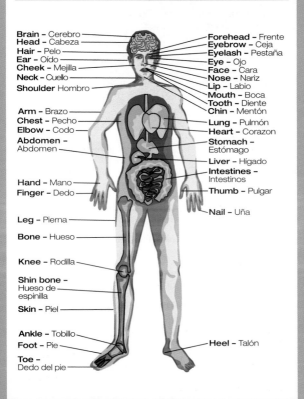

Brain – Cerebro
Head – Cabeza
Hair – Pelo
Ear – Oído
Cheek – Mejilla
Neck – Cuello
Shoulder Hombro

Arm – Brazo
Chest – Pecho
Elbow – Codo
Abdomen – Abdomen

Hand – Mano
Finger – Dedo

Leg – Pierna

Bone – Hueso

Knee – Rodilla

Shin bone – Hueso de espinilla

Skin – Piel

Ankle – Tobillo
Foot – Pie
Toe – Dedo del pie

Forehead – Frente
Eyebrow – Ceja
Eyelash – Pestaña
Eye – Ojo
Face – Cara
Nose – Nariz
Lip – Labio
Mouth – Boca
Tooth – Diente
Chin – Mentón

Lung – Pulmón
Heart – Corazon
Stomach – Estómago
Liver – Hígado
Intestines – Intestinos
Thumb – Pulgar

Nail – Uña

Heel – Talón

FORMS OF ADDRESS
TRATOS

There are two ways of translating the English word 'you'. The formal way is *usted* (which is abbreviated *ud.*). This form of address is a sign of courtesy and respect, and would normally be used when addressing elderly people, teachers, bosses, shopkeepers and people you don't know very well, especially if they are older than you.

The less formal translation of 'you' is *tú*, which is the form generally used when addressing family, friends and people you know well. Nowadays *tú* is used much more often than before, although the *usted* form is very popular in most Latin American countries and is used frequently, especially when speaking to foreigners.

GREETING PEOPLE
SALUDOS

When it comes to greeting each other, the Hispanic people are rather formal, and the usual form of greeting is to shake hands. This applies to both young and old people.

Hugging is also a very Hispanic custom, and men who know each other well will usually hug each other.

Kissing varies from country to country. In Spain a greeting will usually consist of two kisses, one on each cheek, whereas in most Latin American countries there will only be one kiss on the cheek.

Eye contact is important, and Latinos expect you to make eye contact whenever you speak to them. In many societies it is in fact considered rude not to establish and maintain eye contact.

MANNERS
ETIQUETA

The well-known fiery Latin temperament means that Spanish people are usually quite outspoken and direct. This same temperament also leads to rather high levels of noise. The people speak loudly, and the drivers generally hoot a lot, so don't expect an especially quiet time when visiting a Spanish-speaking country!

On the other hand, there is the very Spanish custom of the *siesta*, and in most

Spanish-speaking countries everything comes to a standstill during the hottest part of the day, when people have a rest.

Spanish-speaking people can be very helpful towards strangers. The more you try to talk to them, no matter how excruciating your Spanish pronunciation is, the more they will want to help you. They may even offer to acompany you to whichever place it is you are trying to find. So it would be well worth your while to learn the basics of the language before you embark on a visit to a Spanish-speaking country, whether you are going on holiday or on a business trip. If you make the effort it will be appreciated.

COMMUNICATION
COMUNICACIÓN

There are many Spanish words that cannot be simply and literally translated into English, for example words such as *relación* (relation-ship), *comida* (food) or *paseo* (a walk), which have many more connotations attached to them than their literal meanings tell us.

The Spanish phrase *dar un paseo*, for instance, literally means 'to go for a walk', but it carries with it a wealth of social images such as people out for a leisurely walk with their family and friends, sitting and relaxing at a sidewalk café, seeing people and in turn being seen by others. In Spanish-speaking countries to go for a walk means something entirely different to what it means to English-speaking people.

FOOD AND MEALS
COMIDAS

Just as the geography of the Hispanic world is very extensive, so too is its cuisine. If you talk about Spanish food in the United States of America, you are probably referring to Mexican food. But the food in Mexico is very different from the food in Spain. Many Mexican dishes are based on the tortilla. The Mexican tortilla is a pancake made of maize, whereas the Spanish tortilla is an omelette made of potatoes. In the same way there are many differences between Mexican food and Chilean food, as there are between Chilean food and Argentinian food.

Some kinds of food are common to many Latin American countries. You will be able to find empanadas – snacks made of pastry stuffed with a variety of fillings – in many countries. Some countries are particularly well known for a specific kind of food. Argentina is famous for its beef, and the asado – a range of barbecued meats – is very popular. Dulce de leche, a delicious caramel-like treat, is also found in Argentina. (While you're in Argentina, do try the *mate* – a herbal tea). Chile is known for its superb wine and the wonderful variety of seafood found along the coast. Mention Colombia and the whole world thinks of coffee, just as the mention of Brazil brings to mind feijouada (a pork and black bean stew) and caipirinha (a delicious cocktail that is the national drink of Brazil). El Salvador has pupusas (tortillas with beans, cheese or pork), and in Peru there are more than 2000 kinds of soup. If you are an adventurous eater, Ecuador is the place to go for grilled guinea pig!

Meal times vary enormously from country to country and also from season to season. Dinner is usually quite late – in most cases well after 20:00 and often as late as 22:00 – especially in summer.

OFFICIAL HOLIDAYS
FIESTAS OFICIALES

New Year's Day
Día de Año Nuevo
(1 January)
Exuberant parties and dances are held on 31 December – *la noche de Año Nuevo* – so most people spend New Year's Day recovering.

Epiphany
Día de Reyes
(6 January)
A religious holiday commemorating the manifestation of Christ to the Three Kings.

Easter
Semana Santa
(March/April)
The Easter weekend includes Good Friday – *Viernes Santo* – which is preceded by *Jueves Santo* ('Good Thursday'), as well as Easter Sunday (*Domingo de Pascua*) and Easter Monday (*Lunes Santo*). Special Easter church services are held.

May Day, Labour Day
Fiesta del Trabajo
(1 May)
Labour Day is an official holiday for the workers.

All Saints' Day
Todos los Santos
(1 November)
This is a religious holiday celebrated by Christians to honour all the saints.

Immaculate Conception
La Sagrada Concepción
(8 December)
A religious holiday commemorating the conception of Christ.

Christmas
Navidad
(25 December)
From the first Sunday of Advent private and public festivities mark this special season, leading up to the high-light of Christmas Eve (*Nochebuena*).

REGIONAL FESTIVALS
FIESTAS REGIONALES

Virgen de la Candelaria
(2–8 February)
Puno, Peru.

This is one of the most important annual religious events in Peru. Thousands of musicians and dancers in jewelled costumes and beribboned hats take part in processions parading through the streets of Puno. The same festival is also celebrated in Bolivia, Uruguay, Chile and Venezuela.

Fiesta de San Sebastian de Yumbel
(20 January and 20 March)
Yumbel, Chile.
Every year on these dates thousands of pilgrims journey to Yumbel in Chile's spectacular Lake.

District to participate in the feast day of San Sebastián, the patron saint of archers and soldiers. The celebrations are colourful.

Buenos Aires Tango Festival

(Late February to early March)

Buenos Aires, Argentina.
More than 150 performers gather to give nearly 100 free shows and concerts at this festival also featuring finals of the Metropolitan Ballroom Tango Championship.

Carnaval de Barranquilla

(Mid-February, 4 days before Ash Wednesday)

Barranquilla, Colombia.
This carnival is one of the world's largest. The whole city parties for four days, both day and night, and there is much vibrant music and dancing.

NATIONAL DAYS
FIESTAS NACIONALES

27 February **Dominican Republic**

14 May **Paraguay**

25 May **Argentina**

5 July **Venezuela**

20 July **Colombia**

28 July **Peru**

6 August **Bolivia**

10 August **Ecuador**

25 August **Uruguay**

15 September **Costa Rica, El Salvador, Guatemala, Honduras, Nicaragua**

16 September **Mexico**

18 September **Chile**

12 October **Equatorial Guinea, Spain**

> **SPECIAL FESTIVALS**
> FESTIVALES ESPECIALES

Día de la Raza

(nearest Monday to 12 October)

Columbus Day (Race Day) is celebrated in Argentina, Costa Rica, Ecuador, Honduras, Venezuela, Uruguay, Mexico and Chile, to mark Columbus's discovery of America.

Día de la Cruz

(3 May)

The Day of the Cross is when St Helena is said to have found the cross on which Jesus was crucified. Catholics mount crosses decorated with flowers in their homes. The festival is celebrated in Mexico, Venezuela, El Salvador, and Peru.

Carnaval, Rio de Janeiro

(3 days during February or March – the date varies each year)

The name of Brazil's famous carnival comes from 'carne vale', which means 'goodbye to meat'. People get together for the world's most famous street party to have some fun before Lent, the forty days when Christians are not supposed to eat meat.

People spend all year creating costumes, floats, and dances for the great Samba School Parade.

Noche de Rabanos
(23 December)

Possibly one the strangest of holiday festivals is the Night of the Radishes, which takes place in the city of Oaxaca, Mexico, every year on 23 December. In some parts of Mexico, the radishes grow quite amazingly large. On this day, there is an annual radish sculpture competition. Sculptors carve radishes in the shapes of historical and famous people.

Inti Raymi
(Late June)

This Inca Festival of the Sun celebrates the winter solstice with traditional pageantry, parades, and dances. In Argentina, celebrations take place in towns throughout the northwest on the night before the summer solstice (around 20 June). In Peru, the principal event takes place on 24 June at the Sacsayhuamán ruins and includes the sacrifice of a pair of llamas. In Ecuador, Inti Raymi merges with the fiestas of San Pablo and San Juan to create one big holiday from 24 to 29 June in the Otavalo area.

ENGLISH → SPANISH

A
abbey abadía f
abortion aborto m
about (approximately)
  aproximadamente
above sobre
abroad en el extranjero
abscess absceso m
absolutely por
  supuesto, claro
accelerator
  acelerador m
accent acento m
accept aceptar
accident accidente m
accommodation
  alojamiento m
account cuenta f
accurate exacto
ache dolor m
adapter adaptador m
adhesive tape
  cinta adhesiva f
admission fee
  entrada f
adult (adj, n)
  adulto/a m/f
advance, in advance
  por adelantado
advertisement aviso m
advice consejo m
advise aconsejar
aeroplane avión m
afraid, be afraid of
  tener miedo
after después
afternoon tarde

afterwards después,
  luego
again otra vez
against contra
age edad f
agree estar de acuerdo
agreement acuerdo m
air aire m
air conditioning aire
  acondicionado
air ticket billete aéreo
airmail correo aéreo
airport aeropuerto m
aisle pasillo m
aisle seat asiento en
  el pasillo
all right vale, está bien
allow permitir, dejar
almond almendra f
almost casi
alone solo
already ya
also también
although a pesar de
altogether todo junto
always siempre
a.m. (before noon)
  por la mañana
am, I am yo soy/estoy
amazing fabuloso,
  maravilloso
amber ámbar m
ambulance ambulancia f
among dentro
amount monto m,
  cantidad f
anaesthetic
  anestético m

ancient viejo/a
and y
angry enojado
animal animal m
ankle tobillo m
anniversary aniversario m
annoy molestar
annual anual
another otro/a
answer (n) respuesta f
answer (vb) responder
ant hormiga
antacid antiácido
anybody cualquiera
anything cualquier cosa
apartment piso m, apartemente m
apology disculpa f
appendicitis apendicitis f
appointment cita f
approximately aproximadamente
apron delantal m
are son, están
area barrio m, área f
armchair sillón m
arrange arreglar
arrest arrestar
arrival llegada f
arrive llegar
art arte m
artist artista m/f
ask preguntar
astonishing fascinante
at en
attack (n) ataque m
attack (vb) atacar

attic ático m
audience audiencia f
aunt tía f
auto-teller cajero automático
autumn otoño m
available disponible
avalanche avalancha f
avenue avenida f
average promedio
avoid evitar
awake despertar
away fuera
awful feo/a, malo/a, terrible

B
baby food comida para bebé
back espalda f
backache dolor de espalda
backpack mochila f
bacon tocino m
bad malo/a
bag bolsa f
baggage equipaje m
baggage reclaim recolección de equipajes
bait cebo m, carnada f
bakery panadería f
balcony balcón m
ballpoint pen bolígrafo m, lapicera
Baltic Sea Mar Báltico
bandage venda f, vendaje m

ENGLISH → SPANISH

bar of chocolate
  barra de chocolate
barber's shop
  barbería f
bark (vb) ladrar
barn granero m
barrel barril m
basement sótano m
basket cesta, canasta f
bath bañera f
bathroom baño m
bay bahía f
bay leaf hoja de laurel
be ser, estar
beach playa f
bean haba f, judía f,
  frijol m
beard barba f
beautiful bonito/a,
  precioso/a, lindo/a
beauty salon
  salón de belleza
because porque
because of por
bed cama f
bed & breakfast
  pensión f
bed linen ropa de cama
bedspread cobertor
bee abeja f
beef carne de vaca f
beer cerveza f
before antes
beginner principiante m/f
behind detrás
Belgian (adj, n)
  belga m/f
Belgium Bélgica

believe creer
bell campana f
below bajo
belt cinturón m
bend doblar
beside junto a
bet apostar
better mejor
beyond más allá
bicycle bicicleta f
big gran, grande
bill cuenta f
bin cesto de la basura
binoculars binoculares,
  prismáticos mpl
bird pájaro m, ave f
birth nacimiento m
birth certificate
  certificado de nacimiento
birthday cumpleaños m
birthday card tarjeta
  de cumpleaños
birthday present
  regalo de cumpleaños
biscuit galleta f
bit un poco
bite (vb) morder
black negro/a
blackcurrant
  grosella negra
blanket manta f
bleach (vb) blanquear
bleed sangrar
blind (n) persiana
blind (adj) ciego/a
blister ampolla f
block of flats edificio
  de apartamentos

blocked cerrado/a, bloqueado

blood sangre f

blood pressure presión arterial

blouse blusa f

blow-dry secar

blue azul

blunt contundente

blusher colorete m

boar jabalí m

boarding card tarjeta de embarque

boarding house pensión f

boat barco m, bote m

boat trip viaje en barco

body cuerpo m

boil (n) forúnculo m

boil (vb) hervir

bone hueso m

bonnet (car) capó/ capota m/f

book libro m

bookshop librería f

boots botas fpl

border borde m

boring aburrido, pesado/a

born nacer

borrow tomar prestado

both los dos, ambos

bottle botella f

bottle opener abridor de botellas

bottom (at the) al fondo

bow tie humita, moño

bowl cuenco m

box caja f

boy niño m

boyfriend novio m

bra sostén m

bracelet pulsera f

brake (n) freno m

brake fluid líquido de freno

brake light luz de freno

branch (office) sucursal f

brand marca f

brandy brandy m

bread pan m

break romper

breakable se puede romper, frágil

breakdown (of car) avería f

breakdown van camión de reparación de averías

breakfast desayuno m

break-in robo m

breast pecho m, teta f

breathe respirar

breeze brisa f

brewery fábrica de cerveza

brick ladrillo m

bride novia f

bridegroom novio m

bridge puente m

briefcase maletín m

bright brillante

bring traer

bring in introducir

ENGLISH → SPANISH

brochure folleto m
broken roto/a
bronchitis bronquitis f
brooch broche m
broom escoba f
brother hermano m
brother-in-law
  cuñado m
brown marrón
bruise (n) moretón m
brush cepillo m
Brussels Bruselas
bucket balde, cubo m
buffet car coche
  comedor
buggy cochecito de niño
build construir
building edificio m
bulb (light)
  lamparita f
bulb (plant) bulbo m
bumper
  guardabarros m
bunch manojo m
bureau de change
  oficina de cambio
burglar ladrón/
  ladrona m/f
burglary robo m
burn quemar
burst explotar
bus autobús m
bus stop
  parada de autobús
bush arbusto m
business negocios mpl
business trip
  viaje de negocios

busy ocupado/a
but pero
butcher carnicero/a m/f
butter mantequilla f
butterfly mariposa f
button botón m
buy comprar
by por
bypass (road)
  desviación, carretera de
  circunvalación

C
cab taxi m
cabbage repollo m
cabin cabina f
cable car teleférico m
cake pastel m, torta f
cake shop pastelería f
calculator calculadora f
calf ternera f
call (n) llamada f
call (vb) llamar
calm calma
camp (vb) acampar
camp site
  campamento m
can (n) lata f
can (vb) poder
can opener
  abridor de latas
Canada Canadá
canal canal m
cancel cancelar
cancellation
  cancelación f
cancer cáncer m
candle vela f

candy dulce m
canoe canoa f
cap gorro m
capital (city) capital f
capital (money)
   capital m
car coche, carro, auto m
car ferry transbordador
   de coches
car hire alquiler de
   coches
car insurance
   seguro de coche
car keys
   llaves del coche
car parts partes del
   coche
car wash lavado de
   coches
caravan casa rodante
caravan site
   parque de casa rodante
carburettor
   carburador m
card carta f, tarjeta f
cardboard cartón m
cardigan chaleco m
careful cuidado
caretaker portero/a m/f
carpenter
   carpintero/a m/f
carpet alfombra f
carriage vagón m
carrier bag bolsa f
carrot zanahoria f
carry cargar
carry-cot cuna portable
carton caja f

case caso m
cash efectivo, dinero
   efectivo
cash desk caja f
cash dispenser
   cajero automático
cash register caja f
cashier cajero/a m/f
cassette cassette f
castle castillo m
casualty department
   urgencias
cat gato/a m/f
catch agarrar
cathedral catedral f
Catholic (adj, n)
   católico/a m/f
cauliflower coliflor f
cave cueva f
CD player centro
   musical, toca discos
ceiling cielo raso
celery apio m
cellar bodega f
cemetery cementerio m
Centigrade centígrado
centimetre
   centímetro m
central heating
   calefacción central
central locking
   bloqueo automático
centre centro m
century siglo m
certain certeza
certainly ciertamente,
   claro
certificate certificado m

ENGLISH → SPANISH

ENGLISH → SPANISH

chair silla f
chair lift elevador
de silla
chambermaid
camarera, criada f
champagne champán m
change (n) cambio m
change (vb) cambiar
changing room
vestuario m
channel canal m
chapel capilla f
charcoal carbón m
charge cargar
charge card
tarjeta de crédito
charter flight
vuelo chárter
cheap barato/a
cheap rate
precio barato
cheaper más barato
check registrar
check in registrarse,
inscribirse
cheek mejilla f
Cheers! ¡Salud!
cheese queso m
chef cocinero/a m/f
chemist
farmacéutico/a m/f
cheque cheque m
cheque book
libreta de cheques
cheque card tarjeta de
identidad bancaria
cherry cereza f
chess ajedrez m

chest pecho m
chest of drawers
cómoda f
chestnut castaño m
chewing gum chicle m
chicken pollo m
chicken pox varicela f
child niño/a, chico/a m/f
child car seat asiento
de coche para niños
chimney chimenea f
chin barbilla f, mentón m
China China
china porcelana f
chips papas fritas fpl
chives cebollín
chocolate chocolate m
chocolates
bombones mpl
choir coro m
choose escoger, elegir
chop cortar
Christian name
nombre de pila
Christmas Navidad f
Christmas Eve
Nochebuena f
church iglesia f
cider sidra f
cigar puro m
cigarette cigarrillo m
cigarette lighter
encendedor m
cinema cine m
circle círculo m
cistern cisterna f
citizen ciudadano/a m/f
city ciudad f

city centre centro de la ciudad
class clase f
clean (adj) limpio/a
clean (vb) limpiar
cleaning solution detergente m
cleansing lotion crema limpiadora
clear (adj) claro/a
clever listo/a, inteligente
client cliente m/f
cliff acantilado m
climate clima m
climb subir
cling film plástico para envolver
clinic clínica f
cloakroom baño m
clock reloj m
closed cerrado/a
cloth paño m
clothes ropas fpl
clothes line tendedero m
clothes peg broches para la ropa, pinza f
clothing ropa f
cloud nube f
clutch (car) embrague m
coach autobus m
coal carbón m
coast costa f
coastguard guardia costera
coat abrigo m

coat hanger percha para abrigo
cockroach cucaracha f
cocoa cacao m
coconut coco m
cod bacalao m
code código m
coffee café m
coil (n, contraceptive) espiral f
coil (n, rope) rollo m
coin moneda f
Coke Coca Cola f
colander colador m
cold frío/a
collapse (vb) derrumbarse, colapsar
collar cuello m
collarbone clavícula f
colleague colega m/f
collect recoger, buscar
collect call llamada a cobro revertido
colour color m
colour blind daltónico/a
colour film film a color
comb (n) peine m
comb (vb) peinar
come venir
come back volver, regresar
come in entre
comedy comedia f
comfortable cómodo/a
company compañía f
compartment compartimento m

ENGLISH → SPANISH

compass compás m
complain quejarse
complaint queja f
completely
completamente,
totalmente
composer
compositor/a m/f
compulsory
obligatorio/a
computer ordenador m,
computadora f
concert concierto m
concession concesión f
concussion
conmoción cerebral
condition condición f
condom preservativo,
condón m
conference
conferencia f
confirm confirmar
confirmation
confirmación f
confused confundido/a
Congratulations!
¡Enhorabuena!
¡Felicitaciones!
connecting flight
vuelo de conexión
connection (elec)
conexión f
connection (phone)
instalación f
conscious conciente
constipated
estreñido/a,
constipado/a

consulate consulado m
contact contacto m
contact lenses
lentes de contacto
continue continuar
contraceptive
anticonceptivo m/f
contract contrato m
convenient
conveniente
cook (n) cocinero/a m/f
cook (vb) cocinar
cooker cocina f,
calentador a gas
cookie galleta f
cooking utensils
utensillos de cocina
cool fresco/a
cool bag, cool box
nevera portátil
copy copiar
cork corcho m
corkscrew
sacacorcho m
corner esquina f
correct (adj) correcto/a
corridor pasillo m
cost coste, costo m
cot cuna f
cotton algodón m
cotton wool
algodón hidrófilo
couch sofá m
couchette litera f
cough (n) tos f
cough (vb) toser
cough mixture
jarabe para la tos

Could I? ¿Podría?
¿Puedo?
couldn't no puedo
counter mostrador m
country país m
countryside
campo m, afueras
couple pareja f
courier service servicio
de entrega/courier
course curso m
cousin primo/a m/f
cover charge entrada f
cow vaca f
crab cangrejo m
craft artesanía f
cramp calambre m
crash (vb) chocar
crash helmet casco m
crazy loco/a
cream crema f
crèche guardería de
niños
credit card tarjeta
de crédito
crime delito m
crisps papas fritas fpl
crockery loza, vajilla f
cross (n) cruz m
cross (vb) cruzar
crossing cruce m
crossroads cruce de
caminos
crossword puzzle
crucigrama m
crowd muchedumbre f
crowded lleno/a,
repleto/a

crown corona f
cruise crucero m
crutches muletas fpl
cry llorar
cucumber pepino m
cufflinks gemelos mpl
cup taza f, pocillo m
cupboard armario m,
ropero m
curly rizado/a
currency moneda f
current (n) corriente f
curtain cortina f
cushion almohadón m
custard natillas fpl,
crema pastelera
custom costumbre f
customer cliente m/f
customs aduana f
cut cortar
cutlery cubertería f
cycle (vb) montar/
andar en bicicleta
cycle track sendero de
bicicletas
cyst quiste m
cystitis cistitis f
Czech Republic
República Checa

D
daily diariamente
damage daño m
damp humedad f
dance (vb) bailar
danger peligro m
dangerous peligroso/a
dark oscuro/a

date (appointment) cita f

date (fruit) dátil m

date (of year) fecha f

date of birth fecha de nacimiento

daughter hija f

daughter-in-law nuera f

dawn (n) alba f, amanecer m

day día m

dead muerto/a

deaf sordo/a

deal trato m

dear querido/a

death muerte f

debts deudas fpl

decaffeinated descafeinado/a

December diciembre m

decide decidir

decision decisión f

deck chair silla de patio, tumbona f

deduct descontar

deep profundo/a

definitely definitiva-mente, por supuesto

degree (measure-ment) grado

degree (qualification) título

delay demora f

deliberately deliberadamente

delicious delicioso/a, rico/a

deliver entregar

delivery entrega f

Denmark Dinamarca

dental floss hilo dental

dentist dentista m/f

dentures dentaduras

depart salir

department sección f

department store grandes almacenes mpl, tienda de departamentos

departure salida f

departure lounge sala de embarque

deposit depósito m

describe describir

description descripción f

desert desierto m

desk escritorio m

dessert postre m

destination destino m

details datos, detalles mpl

detergent detergente m

detour desvío m

develop desarrollar

diabetic (adj, n) diabético/a m/f

dial (vb) marcar

dialling code prefijo m

dialling tone señal de marcar, tono

diamond diamante m

diaper pañal m

diarrhoea diarrea f

diary agenda f, diario m

dice dados mpl
dictionary diccionario m
die morir
diesel diesel m
diet dieta f
difference diferencia f
different diferente
difficult difícil
dinghy bote m, lancha neumática
dining room comedor m
dinner cena f
direct (adj) directo/a
direction dirección f
dirty sucio/a
disabled inválido/a
disappear desaparecer
disappointed decepcionado/a
disaster desastre m
disconnected desconectado
discount descuento m
discover descubrir
disease enfermedad f
dish plato m
dishtowel trapo de cocina
dishwasher lavaplatos m
disinfectant desinfectante m
disk disco m
disposable diapers/ nappies pañales descartables
distance distancia f

district barrio m, distrito m
disturb molestar
dive bucear
diving board trampolín m
divorced divorciado
DIY shop ferretería f
dizzy mareado/a
do hacer
doctor médico/a m/f
document documento m
dog perro/a m/f
doll muñeca f
domestic doméstico/a
door puerta f
doorbell timbre m
doorman portero m
double doble
double bed cama doble
double room habitación doble
doughnut donut m
downhill cuesta abajo, barranca abajo
downstairs abajo
dozen docena f
drain (n) desagüe m
draught corriente f
draught beer cerveza de barril/tirada
drawer cajón m
drawing dibujo m
dreadful horrible
dress vestido m
dressing (bandage) vendaje m

ENGLISH → SPANISH

dressing (salad) aliño **m**, vinagreta **f**
dressing gown bata **f**
drill (n) taladro **m**
drink (n) bebida **f**
drink (vb) beber
drinking water agua potable
drive manejar
driver conductor/a **m/f**, chófer **m**
driving licence carnet de conducir, licencia de conductor
drop (n) gota **f**
drug (medicine) medicamento **m**
drug (narcotic) droga **f**
drunk (adj, n) borracho/a **m/f**
dry seco/a
dry cleaner's tintorería **f**
dryer secadora **f**
duck pato/a **m/f**
due pagadero/a, vencimiento/a
dull apagado/a, pesado/a
dummy chupete **m**
during durante
dust polvo **m**
dustbin cubo de la basura
duster paño **m**, trapo **m**
dustpan pala **f**
Dutch, Dutchman, Dutchwoman (adj, n) holandés/holandesa **m/f**

duty-free libre de impuestos
duvet edredón **m**
duvet cover funda para edredón
dye (n) tinte **m**
dye (vb) teñir, colorear
dynamo dínamo **f**

E
each cada
eagle águila **f**
ear oído **m**
earache dolor de oídos
earphones auriculares **mpl**
earrings pendientes, aros **mpl**
earth tierra **f**
earthquake terremoto **m**
east este **m**
Easter Semana Santa
Easter egg huevo de pascua
easy fácil
eat comer
EC Comunidad Europea
economy economía **f**
economy class clase económica
edge borde **m**
eel anguila **f**
egg huevo **m**
either ... or o ... o
elastic elástico/a
elbow codo **m**
electric eléctrico/a

electrician electricista m/f

electricity electricidad f

elevator elevador, asecensor m

embassy embajada f

emergency emergencia f

emergency exit salida de emergencia

empty vacío/a

end final m

engaged (occupied) ocupado/a

engaged (to be married) comprometido/a

engine motor m

engineer ingeniero/a m/f

England Inglaterra

English (language) inglés

English Channel Canal de la Mancha

English, Englishman/ woman (adj, n) inglés/inglesa m/f

enjoy disfrutar

enlargement ampliación f

enough suficiente

enquiry informe m, investigación f

enquiry desk mostrador de información

enter entrar

entrance entrada f

entrance fee entrada f

envelope sobre m

epilepsy epilepsia f

epileptic epiléptico/a

equipment equipo m

error error m

escalator escalera mecánica

escape (vb) escapar

especially especialmente

essential esencial

estate agent agente inmobilario/a

Estonia Estonia

EU Unión Europea

Europe Europa

European (adj, n) europeo/a m/f

even (adj) parejo/a, uniforme

even (adv) hasta

evening tarde f, (early), noche f (late)

eventually finalmente

every cada

everyone cada uno, todos/todas m/f

everything todo

everywhere por todas partes

exactly exactamente

examination examen m

example, for example ejemplo m, por ejemplo

excellent excelente

except excepto

ENGLISH → SPANISH

ENGLISH → SPANISH

excess luggage
exceso de equipaje
exchange (n) cambio,
intercambio m
exciting entusiasmante
exclude excluir
excursion excursión f
excuse (n) disculpa f
Excuse me! ¡Perdón!
exhaust pipe tubo
de escape
exhausted agotado/a
exhibition exposición f
exit salida f
expect esperar
expenses gastos mpl
expensive caro/a
experienced
con experiencia,
experimentado/a
expire caducar, vencer
explain explicar
explosion explosión f
export exportar
exposure exposición f,
revelación f
express (train)
expreso m
extension extensión f
extension lead cable
de extensión
extra extra
extraordinary
extraordinario/a
eye ojo m
eye drops
gotas para los ojos

eye make-up remover
desmaquillador para
ojos
eye shadow sombra
de ojos

F
fabric tejido m
façade fachada f
face cara f
factory fábrica f
faint (vb) desmayarse
fair (fête) feria f
fair (hair colour)
rubio/a
fair (just) justo/a
fairly bastante
fake (adj) falso/a
fake (vb) simular
fall caer
false falso/a
family familia f
famous famoso/a
fan ventilador m
fanbelt correa del
ventilador
far (adj) lejano/a
far (adv) lejos
fare tarifa f
farm granja f
farmer granjero/a m/f
farmhouse cortijo m,
hacienda f
fashionable de moda
fast rápido/a
fasten abrochar,
ajustar

fasten seatbelt ajustar el cinturón de seguridad
fat gordo/a
father padre m
father-in-law suegro m
fatty graso/a
fault defecto m, culpa f
faulty defectuoso/a
favourite favorito/a
fax facsímil, fax
February febrero m
feed (vb) alimentar
feel sentir
feet pies mpl
female mujer f
fence alambrada f
fender parachoques m, guardabarros m
ferry transbordador m, ferry m
festival festival m
fetch buscar, traer
fever fiebre f
few, a few pocos/as m/f
fiancé, fiancée novio/a, prometido/a m/f
field campo m
fight (n) pelea, lucha f
fight (vb) luchar, pelear
file (folder) archivo m, carpeta f
file (tool) lima f
fill, fill in, fill up llenar
fillet filete m
filling (sandwich) relleno m

filling (tooth) empaste m
film (n) película f
film (vb) filmar
film processing revelado
filter filtro m
filthy mugriento/a
find encontrar
fine (adj) fino/a
fine (n) multa f
finger dedo m
finish (vb) terminar
fire fuego m
fire brigade bomberos mpl
fire exit salida de emergencia
fire extinguisher extinguidor de fuego
first, at first primero/a, al principio
first aid primeros auxilios
first-aid kit maletín de primeros auxilios
first class primera clase
first floor primer piso m
first name primer nombre, nombre de pila
fish pescado m
fishing permit permiso de pesca
fishing rod caña de pescar

ENGLISH → SPANISH

fishmonger's pescadería **f**
fit (healthy) en forma
fitting room cambiador **m**
fix arreglar, reparar
fizzy con gas
flannel franela **f**
flash (of lightning) relámpago
flashlight linterna eléctrica
flask termo **m**
flat (n) apartamento **m**, piso **m**
flat battery batería descargada
flat tyre neumático sin aire
flavour sabor **m**
flaw desperfecto **m**, imperfección **f**
flea pulga **f**
flight vuelo **m**
flip flops chancletas **fpl**
flippers aletas **fpl**
flood inundación **f**
floor (of room) suelo **m**
floor (storey) piso **m**
floorcloth trapo/paño para el suelo
florist florista **m/f**
flour harina **f**
flower flor **f**
flu gripe **f**
fluent con fluidez
fly (vb) volar
fog niebla, neblina **f**

folk gente **f**
follow seguir
food alimento **m**, comida **f**
food poisoning comida envenenada
food shop almacén **m**, tienda **f**
foot pie **m**
football fútbol **m**
football match partido/ juego de fútbol
footpath sendero **m**
for por, para
forbidden prohibido/a
forehead frente **f**
foreign raro/a
foreign, foreigner (adj, n) extranjero/a **m/f**
forest bosque **m**
forget olvidar
fork tenedor **m**
form (document) formulario **m**
form (shape) forma **f**
formal formal, educado/a
fortnight quincena **f**
fortress fuerte **m**
fortunately por suerte
fountain fuente **f**
four-wheel drive cuatro por cuatro
fox zorro/a **m/f**
fracture fractura **f**
frame marco **m**
France Francia
free libre

freelance por su cuenta, independiente
freeway autopista f
freezer congelador m
French, Frenchman/ woman (adj, n) francés/francesa m/f
French fries papas fritas fpl
frequent frecuente
fresh fresco/a
Friday viernes m
fridge nevera f, refrigerador m
fried frito/a
friend amigo/a m/f
friendly amigable, simpático/a
frog rana f
from (origin) de
from (time) desde
front frente m
frost helada f
frozen congelado/a
fruit fruta f
fruit juice jugo de fruta
fry freír
frying pan sartén f
fuel combustible m
fuel gauge indicador de combustible
full lleno/a
full board pensión completa
fun (adj) divertido/a
fun (n) diversión f
funeral funeral m
funicular funicular m

funny gracioso/a
fur piel f
fur coat abrigo de piel
furnished amueblado
furniture muebles mpl
further más allá
fuse fusible m
fuse box caja de fusibles
future futuro m

G

Gallery galería f
gallon galón m
game juego m
garage garaje m
garden jardín m
garlic ajo m
gas gas, combustible m
gas cooker hornalla f, calentador a gas
gate puerta f
gay gay, homosexual
gay bar bar gay
gear equipo m, ropa f
gear lever palanca de cambios
gearbox caja de cambios
general general
generous generoso/a
Geneva Ginebra
gents' toilet baño de hombres
genuine auténtico/a, genuino/a, real
German (adj, n) alemán, alemana m/f

German measles
rubeola f
Germany Alemania
get obtener
get off bajar
get on subir
get up levantarse
gift regalo m
girl niña f
girlfriend novia f
give dar
give back devolver
glacier glaciar m
glad encantado/a
glass (tumbler) vaso m
glasses (spectacles)
lentes m/f, gafas fpl,
anteojos mpl
gloomy apagado/a
gloves guantes mpl
glue pegamento m
go ir
go (by car) manejar,
ir en coche
go (on foot) andar
go away irse
go back volver
goat cabra f
God Dios m
goggles gafas
protectoras
gold oro m
golf club (place) club
de golf
golf club (stick) palo
de golf
golf course campo
de golf

good bueno/a
good afternoon
buenas tardes
good day buenos días
good evening buenas
tardes (if still light)
Good Friday Viernes
Santo
good luck buena suerte
good morning
buenos días
good night
buenas noches
goodbye adiós
goose ganso m
Gothic gótico/a
government gobierno m
gradually poco a poco,
gradualmente
gram gramo m
grammar gramática f
grand grandioso/a
granddaughter nieta f
grandfather abuelo m
grandmother abuela f
grandparents
abuelos mpl
grandson nieto m
grapes uvas fpl
grass césped m
grated rallado/a
grateful agradecido/a
gravy salsa f
greasy graso/a
great gran, grande,
vasto/a, importante
Great Britain
Gran Bretaña

Greece Grecia
Greek (adj, n)
  griego/a m/f
green verde
greengrocer's
  verdulería
greeting saludo m
grey gris
grilled a la parrilla
ground tierra f
ground floor
  planta baja
group grupo m
guarantee garantía f
guard guardia m/f
guest huésped/a m/f
guesthouse pensión f
guide guía m/f
guide book
  guía de turismo
guided tour
  visita guiada
guitar guitarra f
gun arma f
gym gimnasio m

H
hail granizo m
hair cabello m, pelo m
hairbrush
  cepillo de pelo
haircut corte de pelo
hairdresser
  peluquero/a m/f
hairdresser's
  peluquería f
hairdryer secador
  de pelo

half (adj) medio/a,
half (n) mitad f
hall sala f
ham jamón m
hamburger
  hamburguesa f
hammer martillo m
hand mano f
hand luggage
  equipaje de mano
handbag bolso m,
  cartera f
handbrake
  freno de mano
handicapped
  minusválido/a
handkerchief pañuelo m
handle mango m,
  palanca f
handmade
  hecho a mano
handsome guapo/a
hang up (phone)
  colgar
hanger percha f
hang-gliding vuelo libre,
  aladeltismo
hangover resaca f
happen pasar
happy feliz
Happy Easter!
  ¡Feliz Semana Santa!
Happy New Year!
  ¡Feliz Año Nuevo!
harbour puerto m
hard duro/a
hard disk disco duro
hardly apenas

ENGLISH → SPANISH

ENGLISH → SPANISH

hardware shop
ferretería f
harvest cosecha f
hat sombrero m
have tener
have to deber,
tener que
hay fever
fiebre del heno
hazelnut avellana f
he él
head cabeza f
headache
dolor de cabeza
headlight/s faro m,
luces delanteras
headphones
auriculares mpl
health food shop
tienda de alimentos
naturales
healthy saludable
hear oír, escuchar
hearing aid audífono m
heart corazón m
heart attack
ataque al corazón
heartburn acidez f
heat calor m
heater calefactor m
heating calefacción f
heavy pesado/a
heel talón m
height altura f
helicopter helicóptero m
helmet casco m
Help! ¡Ayuda!
help (vb) ayudar

hem dobladillo m,
basta
her su
herbal tea té de
hierbas, té natural
herbs hierbas fpl
here aquí, acá
hernia hernia f
hide esconder
high alto/a
high blood pressure
presión alta (sangre)
high chair silla alta
him, to him él, a él
hip cadera f
hip replacement
reemplazo de cadera
hire (vb) alquilar
hire car coche de
alquiler
his su
historic histórico/a
history historia f
hit golpear
hitchhike hacer
autostop, hacer dedo
hold tener
hole hueco m, hoyo m,
agujero m
holidays vacaciones fpl
holy sagrado/a
home casa f
homesickness
echar de menos
homosexual
homosexual
honest honrado/a
honey miel f

honeymoon
luna de miel
hood (car) capó/
capota m/f
hood (garment)
capucha f
hope esperanza f
hopefully ojalá
horn (animal) cuerno m
horn (car) bocina f
horse caballo m
horse racing
carrera de caballos
horse riding
paseo a caballo
hose pipe manguera f
hospital hospital m
hospitality hospitalidad f
hostel parador m,
albergue m
hot caliente
hot spring termas fpl
hot-water bottle
bolsa de agua caliente
hour hora f
hourly (adj) cada hora
hourly (adv) por horas
house casa f
house wine
vino de la casa
housework trabajo
doméstico, tarea f
hovercraft
hidrodeslizador m
How? ¿Cómo?
How are you?
¿Cómo estás?

How do you do?
¿Qué tal? ¿Cómo
estás?
How many?
¿Cuánto/a?
How much is it?
¿Cuánto es?
humid húmedo/a
humour humor m
Hungarian (adj, n)
húngaro/a m/f
Hungary Hungría
hungry con hambre
hunt cazar
hunting permit
permiso de caza
hurry (vb) apurarse
hurt (vb) doler
hurts duele
husband marido,
esposo m
hydrofoil hidroala f
hypodermic needle
aguja hipodérmica

I
I yo
ice hielo m
ice cream helado m
ice rink pista de hielo
ice skates patines mpl
iced coffee café
helado m
idea idea f
identity card carné de
identidad, tarjeta de
identidad, documento
de identidad

ENGLISH → SPANISH

if si
if not si no
ignition encendido **m**
ignition key
llave de contacto, llave
de encendido
ill enfermo/a
illness enfermedad **f**
immediately
inmediatamente
important importante
impossible imposible
improve mejorar
in en
inch pulgada **f**
included incluido
inconvenience
inconveniente **f**
incredible increíble
Indian (adj, n)
indio/a **m/f**
indicator indicador
de giro, intermitente **m**
indigestion indigestión **f**
indoor pool piscina
climatizada/cubierta
indoors a puertas
adentro
infection infección **f**
infectious infeccioso/a
inflammation
inflamación **f**
inflate inflar
informal informal
information
información **f**
ingredients
ingredientes **mpl**

injection inyección **f**
injured lastimado/a,
herido/a
injury herida **f**
ink tinta **f**
in-laws suegros **mpl**
inn posada **f**
inner tube tubo interno,
cámara de aire
insect insecto **m**
insect bite
picadura de insecto
insect repellent
repelente de insectos
inside dentro, adentro
insist insistir
insomnia insomnio **m**
inspect registrar
instant coffee
café instantáneo
instead en lugar de
insulin insulina **f**
insurance seguro **m**
intelligent inteligente
intend significar
interesting interesante
international
internacional
interpreter
intérprete **m/f**
intersection cruce **m**
interval intervalo **m**
into en
introduce introducir,
presentar (people)
investigation
investigación **f**
invitation invitación **f**

invite invitar
invoice factura f
Ireland Irlanda
Irish, Irishman/woman (adj, n) irlandés/irlandesa m/f
iron (n, appliance) plancha f
iron (n, metal) hierro m
iron (vb) planchar
ironing board tabla de planchar
ironmonger's ferretería f
is es/está
island isla f
it (direct object) lo/la
it (indirect object) le
it (subject) él/ella/ello
Italian (adj, n) italiano/a m/f
Italian (language) italiano
Italy Italia
itch (n) picazón
itch (vb) picar

J

jack (car) gato m
jacket chaqueta f, abrigo m
jam jalea f, mermelada f
jammed tapado
January enero m
jar frasco m
jaundice ictericia f
jaw mandíbula f
jealous celoso/a

jelly jalea f
jellyfish medusa, aguamala f
jersey jersey m
Jew, Jewish (n, adj) judío/a m/f
jeweller's joyería f
jewellery joyas fpl
job trabajo m
jog (n) trote m
jog (vb) correr, trotar
join unirse, asociarse
joint juntura f
joke broma f
journey travesía f, viaje m
joy alegría f
judge juez m/f
jug jarra f
juice zumo m, jugo m
July julio m
jump (n) salto m
jump (vb) saltar
jump leads cables de conexion de batería
jumper súeter, jersey m
junction cruce m
June junio m
just (fair) justo/a
just (only) solamente

K

keep guardar
Keep the change! ¡Guarde el cambio!
kettle hervidor m
key llave f
key ring llavero m
kick patear

ENGLISH → SPANISH

kidney riñón m
kill matar
kilo kilo m
kilogram kilogramo m
kilometre kilómetro m
kind amable
king rey m
kiosk quiosco m
kiss (n) beso m
kiss (vb) besar
kitchen cocina f
kitchenette cocinita f
knee rodilla f
knickers bragas fpl
knife cuchillo m
knit tejer
knitting needle
    aguja de tejer
knitwear tejido m
knock golpear
knock down derribar
knock over atropellar
know saber, conocer

L
label etiqueta f
lace puntilla f
ladder escalera f
ladies' toilet
    baño de mujeres
ladies' wear
    ropa de mujer
lady dama f, mujer f,
    señora f
lager cerveza rubia
lake lago m
lamb cordero m
lamp lámpara f

land tierra f
landlady propietaria f
landlord propietario m
landslide
    desprendimiento
    de tierras
lane carril m
language lengua f,
    idioma m
language course
    curso de idioma
large gran, grande
last último/a
last night anoche
late tarde
later luego, más tarde
Latvia Latvia
laugh (n) risa f
laugh (vb) reír
launderette,
    laundromat
    lavandería automática
laundry lavandería f
lavatory baño m
law ley f
lawyer abogado/a m/f
laxative (adj, n)
    laxante m
lazy perezoso/a, vago/a
lead (n, metal) plomo
lead (vb) llevar
lead-free sin plomo
leaf hoja f
leaflet folleto m
leak (n) agujero m
leak (vb) gotear
learn aprender

lease (n) contrato
de alquiler
lease (vb) arrendar
leather piel f, cuero m
leave salir, dejar
leek puerro m
left, to the left
izquierdo/a,
a la izquierda
left-hand drive
conducción a la
izquierda
left-handed zurdo/a
leg pierna f
lemon limón m
lemonade limonada f
lend prestar
lens lente f
lenses lentes m/f
lentil lenteja f
lesbian (adj, n)
lesbiana f
less menos
lesson lección f, clase f
let (vb, allow) dejar,
permitir
let (vb, hire) alquilar
letter carta f
letterbox buzón m
lettuce lechuga f
level crossing
cruce a nivel
lever palanca f
library biblioteca f
licence licencia f,
permiso m
lid tapa f
lie (n, untruth) mentira f

lie (vb, fib) mentir
lie down acostarse
life vida f
life belt cinturón
salvavidas
life insurance
seguro de vida
life jacket chaleco
salvavidas
lifeguard socorrista m/f
lift (n, elevator)
elevador, ascensor m
lift (vb) levantar
light (adj, colour)
claro/a
light (adj, weight)
ligero/a, liviano/a
light (n) luz f
light (vb) iluminar
light bulb bombita f,
lamparita f
lightning rayo m
like (prep) como
like (vb) gustar
lime lima f
line línea f
linen lino m
lingerie ropa interior
lion león m
lipstick lápiz de labios
liqueur licor m
list lista f
listen escuchar
Lithuania Lituania
litre litro m
litter (n) basura f
litter (vb) ensuciar
little pequeño/a

ENGLISH → SPANISH

live vivir
lively vivo/a
liver hígado m
living room sala de estar
loaf barra f, pan m
lobby vestíbulo m
lobster langosta f
local local
lock (n) cerradura f
lock (vb) cerrar
lock in guardar en el armario
lock out cerrar, dejar encerrado
locked in bajo llave
locker armario m
lollipop chupetín
long (adj, size) largo/a
long (adj, time) mucho/a
long-distance call llamada de larga distancia
look after cuidar
look at mirar
look for buscar
look forward to esperar con ilusión
loose suelto/a
lorry camioneta f
lose perder
lost perdido/a
lost property propiedad perdida
lot mucho/a
loud ruidoso/a
lounge sala de estar, salón m

love (n) amor m
love (vb) amar
lovely precioso/a
low bajo/a
low fat bajas calorías
luck suerte f
luggage equipaje m
luggage rack portaequipaje m
luggage tag etiqueta f
luggage trolley carrito para equipaje
lump terrón m, trozo m
lunch almuerzo m
lung pulmón m
Luxembourg Luxemburgo
luxury lujo m

M
machine máquina f
mad loco/a
made hecho/a
magazine revista f
maggot gusano m
magnet imán m
magnifying glass lupa f
maid sirvienta, mucama f
maiden name nombre de soltera
mail (n) correo m
mail (vb) enviar por correo
main principal
main course plato principal

main post office
correo central
main road
calle principal/mayor
mains switch
interruptor principal
make hacer
male masculino
man hombre m
man-made fibre
fibra sintética
manager gerente m/f
manual (adj, n)
manual m
many muchos/as
map mapa m
marble mármol m
March marzo m
market mercado m
marmalade mermelada f
married casado/a
marsh pantano m
mascara rímel m
mashed potatoes
puré de papas
mask máscara f
Mass (rel) misa f
mast mástil m
match (sport) partido m
matches (for lighting)
fósforos mpl
material tejido m
matter asunto m
matter – it doesn't
matter no importa
mattress colchón f
May mayo m
may poder

maybe quizás, tal vez
mayonnaise mayonesa f
me, to me a mí, para mí
meal comida f
mean (intend) significar
mean (nasty) malo/a
measles sarampión m
measure (n) medida f
measure (vb) medir
meat carne f
mechanic
mecánico/a m/f
medical insurance
seguro médico
medicine (drug)
medicamento m
medicine (science)
medicina f
medieval medieval
Mediterranean
mediterráneo/a
medium mediano/a
medium dry wine
vino medio seco
medium rare (meat)
carne medio hecha
medium sized
talla media
meet encontrar
meeting reunión f
melon melón m
melt derretir
men hombres
mend remendar
meningitis meningitis
menswear
ropa de hombre
mention mencionar

ENGLISH → SPANISH

menu menú m
meringue merengue m
message recado,
   mensaje m
metal metal m
meter contador m
metre metro m
metro metro m
microwave oven
   micro ondas m
midday mediodía m
middle medio m
midnight medianoche f
might (vb) poder
migraine migraña f
milk leche f
minced meat
   carne picada
mind mente f
mineral water
   agua mineral
minister ministro/a m/f
mint menta f
minute minuto m
mirror espejo m
Miss señorita f
missing perdido/a,
   desaparecido/a
mist neblina f
mistake error m
misunderstanding
   malentendido m
mix (vb) mezclar
mix-up (n) confusión f
mix up (vb) confundir
mobile phone
   teléfono móvil

moisturizer
   crema hidratante
moment momento m
monastery
   monasterio m
Monday lunes m
money dinero m
money belt monedero m
money order giro m
month mes m
monthly mensualmente
monument
   monumento m
moon luna f
mooring amarradero m
more más
morning mañana f
mosque mezquita f
mosquito mosquito m
most la mayoría de
mostly generalmente
moth polilla f
mother madre f
mother-in-law suegra f
motor motor m
motorbike motocicleta f
motorboat lancha f
motorway autopista f
mountain montaña f
mountain rescue
   rescate de montaña
mountaineering
   montañismo m
mouse ratón m
moustache bigote m
mouth boca f
mouth ulcer
   úlcera de boca

mouthwash
desinfectante bucal
move mover,
move house mudarse
de casa
Mr señor m
Mrs señora f
Ms señorita f
much mucho/a
mud barro m
mug taza m
mugged robado
mumps paperas fpl
muscle músculo m
museum museo m
mushroom hongo m,,
champiñon m
musician músico/a m/f
Muslim musulmán/
musulmana m/f
mussel mejillón m
must deber
mustard mostaza f
mutton cordero m
my mi
myself yo mismo

N
nail uña f
nail brush cepillo
de uñas
nail file lima de uñas
nail polish/varnish
pintura de uñas, esmalte
de uñas
nail polish remover
quitaesmalte

nail scissors
tijeras para uñas
name nombre m
nanny niñera f
napkin servilleta f
nappy pañal m
narrow angosto/a,
estrecho/a
nasty malo/a, sucio/a,
indecente
national nacional
nationality nacionalidad f
natural natural
nature naturaleza f
nature reserve
reserva natural
nausea náusea f
navy armada f
navy blue azul marino
near (adj) cercano/a
near (adv) cerca
nearby (adj) cercano/a
nearby (adv) cerca, en
los alrededores
nearly casi
necessary necesario/a
neck cuello m
necklace collar m
need (n) necesidad f
need (vb) necesitar
needle aguja f
negative (n, photo)
negativo m
neighbour vecino/a m/f
neither ... nor ni ... ni
nephew sobrino m
nest nido m
net red f

ENGLISH → SPANISH

ENGLISH → SPANISH

Netherlands Países Bajos
never nunca
new nuevo/a
New Year Año Nuevo
New Year's Eve Noche de Año Nuevo
New Zealand, New Zealander Nueva Zelanda, neocelandés
news noticias fpl
news stand quiosco m
newspaper periódico m
next próximo/a
nice agradable
niece sobrina f
night, last night noche f, anoche
nightdress vestido de noche
no no
nobody nadie
noise ruido m
noisy ruidoso/a
non-alcoholic sin alcohol
non-smoking no fumador/a
none ninguno/a
north norte m
North Sea Mar del Norte
Northern Ireland Irlanda del Norte
Norway Noruega
Norwegian (adj, n) noruego/a m/f
nose nariz f

not no
note nota f
notebook cuaderno m
notepaper papel de carta
nothing nada
nothing else nada más
noticeboard cartelera de avisos
novel novela f
November noviembre m
now ahora
nudist beach playa nudista
number número m
number plate matrícula f
nurse enfermero/a m/f
nursery (plants) vivero m
nursery school guardería infantil, jardín de infantes
nursery slope pistas para principiantes
nut nuez f
nut (for bolt) tornillo m

O
oak roble m
oar remo m
oats avena f
obtain obtener
occasionally de vez en cuando, cada tanto
occupation ocupación f
occupied (e.g. toilet) ocupado/a

ocean océano m
October octubre m
odd (number) impar
odd (strange) raro/a
of de
off de
office oficina f
often con frecuencia
oil aceite m
ointment pomada f
OK bien, claro
old viejo/a
old-age pensioner
 jubilado/a m/f
old-fashioned
 pasado/a de moda
olive aceituna f
olive oil aceite de oliva
omelette tortilla f
on en, sobre
once una vez
one uno m
one-way street
 calle de una sola mano
onion cebolla f
only (adj) solamente
only (adv) sólo
open abierto/a
open ticket billete
 abierto
opening times horario
 de apertura
opera ópera f
operation operación f
operator (phone)
 operador/a m/f
ophthalmologist
 oculista m/f

opposite opuesto/a
optician óptico/a m/f
or o
orange naranja f
orange juice
 jugo de naranja
orchestra orquesta f
order (n) orden m
order (vb) pedir
organic vegetables
 verduras orgánicas
other otro/a
otherwise de otra
 forma, si no
our nuestro/a
out fuera, afuera
out of order
 no funciona
outdoors al aire libre
outside fuera, afuera
outskirts afueras
oven horno m
ovenproof resistente
 al horno
over sobre
over here acá, aquí
over there allá
overcharge cobrar
 excesivamente
overcoat abrigo m
overdone muy hecho
overheat recalentar
overnight por la noche,
 durante la noche
overtake adelantar
owe deber
owl lechuza f

ENGLISH → SPANISH

owner propietario/a, dueño/a m/f

P

pacemaker marcapasos m
pacifier chupete m
pack (vb) empacar
package paquete m
package holiday vacaciones organizadas
packet paquete m
padlock candado m
page página f
paid pagado/a
pail balde, cubo m
pain dolor m
painful doloroso/a
painkiller mitigador, medicina para el dolor, analgésico m
paint (vb) pintar
paint (n) pintura f
painting cuadro m
pair par m
palace palacio m
pale pálido/a
pan cacerola f
pancake panqueque m
panties bragas fpl
pants pantalones mpl
pantyhose panty m
paper papel m
paper napkins servilletas de papel
parcel paquete m
Pardon? ¿Qué? ¿Disculpa? ¿Cómo?

parents padres mpl
parents-in-law suegros mpl
park (n) parque m
park (vb) aparcar, estacionar
parking disc disco de aparcamiento/ estacionamiento
parking fine multa f
parking meter parquímetro m
parking ticket boleto de estacionamiento
part parte f
partner (companion) compañero/a m/f
partner (business) socio/a m/f
party (celebration) fiesta f
party (political) partido m
pass (vb) pasar
pass control control de pasaporte
passenger pasajero/a m/f
passport pasaporte m
past pasado m
pastry pastel m
path sendero m
patient (adj, n) paciente m/f
pattern patrón m
pavement calzada, vereda f
pay pagar

payment pago m
payphone teléfono pago/público
pea arveja f, chícharo m
peach durazno m
peak pico m
peak rate precio de temporada alta
peanut maní m
pear pera f
pearl perla f
peculiar peculiar
pedal pedal m
pedestrian peatón m
pedestrian crossing paso de peatones
peel (n) piel f
peel (vb) pelar
peg broche m
pen lapicera, boli m
pencil lápiz m
penfriend amigo/a invisible, amigo/a por carta
peninsula península f
people gente f
pepper (vegetable) pimiento m
pepper (spice) pimienta f
per por
perfect perfecto/a
performance representación f
perfume perfume m
perhaps quizás, tal vez
period período m
perm permanente f

permit (n) permiso m
permit (vb) permitir
person persona f
pet animal doméstico
petrol combustible m
petrol can contenedor de combustible
petrol station estación de servicio
pharmacist farmacéutico/a m/f
pharmacy farmacia f
phone teléfono m
phone booth cabina telefónica
phone card tarjeta de llamadas
phone number número de teléfono
photo foto f
photocopy (n) fotocopia f
photograph (n) fotografía f
photograph (vb) fotografiar
phrase book libro de frases
piano piano m
pickpocket carterista f, ratero/a m/f
picnic picnic m, comida de campo
picture foto f
picture frame marco de foto
pie empanada f
piece pieza f, pedazo m

ENGLISH → SPANISH

121

ENGLISH → SPANISH

pig cerdo m, chancho
pill pastilla f
pillow almohada f
pillowcase funda para almohada
pilot piloto m
pin alfiler m
pin number número de clave
pineapple piña f, ananá m
pink rosa
pipe (plumbing) cañería f
pipe (smoking) pipa f
pity, It's a pity! pena f, ¡Qué pena!
place lugar m
plain simple
plait trenza f
plane avión m
plant planta f
plaster yeso m
plastic plástico/a
plastic bag bolsa de plástico
plate plato m
platform plataforma f, andén m
play (n, theatre) obra f
play (vb, game) jugar
playground patio de recreo
please por favor
pleased encantado/a
Pleased to meet you! ¡Encantado!

plenty suficiente demasiado
pliers alicates mpl, tenazas fpl
plug (bath) tapón m
plug (elec) enchufe m
plum ciruela f
plumber plomero/a m/f
p.m. (after noon) por la tarde
poached escalfado
pocket bolsillo m
point (n) punto m
point (vb) señalar
points (car) platinos mpl
poison veneno m
poisonous venenoso/a
Poland Polonia
Pole, Polish (n, adj) polaco/a m/f
police policía f
police station estación de policía, comisaría f
policeman/woman agente de policía
polish (n) cera f
polish (vb) pulir
polite respetuoso/a, educado/a
polluted contaminado
pool piscina f
poor (impecunious) pobre
poor (quality) malo/a
poppy amapola f
popular popular
population población f
pork carne de cerdo

port (n, harbour) puerto m
port (n, wine) oporto m
porter portero/a m/f
portion porción, parte f
portrait retrato m
Portugal Portugal
Portuguese (adj, n) portugués/ portuguesa m/f
posh elegante
possible posible
post (n) correo m
post (vb) enviar por correo
post office oficina de correos
post office box casilla de correo
postage franqueo m
postage stamp estampilla f
postal code código postal
postbox buzón m
postcard postal f
poster póster m
postman/postwoman cartero/a m/f
postpone aplazar
potato papa f
pothole bache m
pottery cerámica f
pound libra f
pour servir
powder polvo m
powdered milk leche en polvo

power cut corte de electricidad
practice práctica f
practise practicar
pram cochecito m
prawn gamba f
pray rezar
prefer preferir
pregnant embarazada
prescription receta f
present (adj) presente
present (n) regalo m
present (vb) regalar
pressure presión f
pretty bonito/a
price precio m
priest cura m
prime minister primer/a ministro/a m/f
print (vb) imprimir
printed matter asunto escrito, impresos mpl
prison cárcel f
private privado/a
prize premio m
probably probablemente
problem problema m
programme, program programa m
prohibited prohibido/a
promise (n) promesa f
promise (vb) prometer
pronounce pronunciar
properly correctamente
Protestant protestante m/f
public público/a

public holiday día feriado, fiesta nacional
pudding postre m
pull tirar
pullover pullover m, chaleco m
pump (vb) inflar
puncture pinchazo m
puppet show espectáculo de marionetas
purple morado/a
purse bolso m, monedero m
push empujar
pushchair silla de ruedas
put poner
put up with aguantar
pyjamas pijamas m

Q
quality calidad f
quantity cantidad f
quarantine cuarentena f
quarrel (n) riña f
quarrel (vb) pelear, discutir
quarter cuarto m
quay muelle m
queen reina f
question pregunta f, cuestión f
queue (n) cola f
queue (vb) hacer cola
quickly rápidamente
quiet tranquilo/a, quieto

quilt edredón
quite completamente

R
rabbit conejo/a m/f
rabies rabia f
race (people) raza f
race (sport) carrera f
race course hipódromo m
racket raqueta f
radiator radiador m
radio radio f
radish rábano m
rag trapo m
railway ferrocarril m
railway station estación de tren, estación de ferrocarril
rain lluvia f
raincoat impermeable m
raisin pasa f
rake rastrillo m
rape (n) violación f
rape (vb) violar
rare raro/a
rash erupción m
raspberry frambuesa f
rat rata f
rate (of exchange) tipo de cambio
raw crudo/a
razor hoja de afeitar
razor blade hoja de afeitar
read leer
ready listo/a
real real

realize darse cuenta

really realmente

rear-view mirror espejo retrovisor

reasonable razonable

receipt recibo m

receiver (tax) recaudador/a m/f

receiver (telephone) auricular m

recently recientemente

reception recepción f

receptionist recepcionista m/f

recharge recargar

recipe receta f

recognize reconocer

recommend recomendar

record (n, legal) documento m

record (n, music) disco m

red rojo/a

red wine vino tinto

redcurrant grosella roja

reduce reducir

reduction reducción f

refund (n) reembolso m

refund (vb) devolver, reembolsar

refuse (n) basura f

refuse (vb) rechazar

region región f

register (n) registro m

register (vb) certificar

registered mail correo certificado

registration form formulario de inscripción

registration number número de inscripción

relative, relation pariente m/f

remain quedarse

remember recordar

rent (vb) alquilar

repair (n) reparación f

repair (vb) reparar

repeat repetir

reply (n) respuesta f

reply (vb) contestar

report (n) informe m

report (vb) informar

request (n) petición f, pedido m, solicitud f

request (vb) pedir

require requerir

rescue (n) rescate m

rescue salvar

reservation reserva f

reserve reservar

resident (adj, n) residente m/f

resort complejo turístico

rest (relax) descansar

rest (remainder) resto m

retired jubilado/a, retirado/a

return regresar, volver

return ticket billete de ida y vuelta

reverse (n) revés m

ENGLISH → SPANISH

reverse (vb) dar marcha atrás
reverse gear marcha atrás
reverse-charge call llamada de cobro revertido
revolting asqueroso/a
rheumatism reuma **m**
rib costilla **f**
ribbon cinta **f**
rice arroz **m**
rich rico/a
ride montar
ridiculous ridículo/a
right derecho/a
right-hand drive conducción a la derecha
ring (n) anillo **m**
ring (vb) sonar
ring road camino circular
rip-off estafa **f**
ripe maduro/a
river río **m**
road calle **f,** camino **m,** carretera **f**
road accident accidente de tráfico
road map mapa de carreteras
road sign señal de tráfico
road works carretera en obras
roll darse vuelta
roof techo **m**
roof-rack portaequipaje **m**

room cuarto **m,** habitación **f**
rope soga, cuerda **f**
rose (flower) rosa **f**
rotten podrido/a
rough áspero/a
roughly aproximadamente
round redondo/a
roundabout rotonda **f**
row (n) fila **f**
row (vb) remar
royal real
rubber caucho **m,** goma **f**
rubbish basura **f**
rubella rubeola **f**
rudder timón **m**
rug alfombra **f**
ruin ruina **f**
ruler (for measuring) regla **f**
rum ron **m**
run correr
rush darse prisa, apurarse
rusty oxidado/a
rye bread pan de centeno

S
sad triste
saddle silla de montar
safe (adj) seguro
safe (n) caja fuerte
safety belt cinturón de seguridad
safety pin imperdible **m**

sail navegar
sailing navegación f
salad ensalada f
salad dressing
  condimento para
  ensalada, vinagreta f
sale rebajas, ofertas fpl,
  liquidación f
sales representative
  representante de ventas
salesperson
  vendedor/a m/f
salmon salmón m
salt sal f
same mismo/a, igual
sand arena f
sandals sandalias,
  ojotas fpl
sandwich sandwich m
sanitary pads
  compresa higiénica
Saturday sábado m
sauce salsa f
saucer platillo m
sausage salchicha f
save ahorrar
savoury salado/a
say decir
scales balanza f
scarf bufanda f
scenery paisaje m
school escuela f
scissors tijeras fpl
Scot, Scottish (n, adj)
  escocés/escocesa m/f
Scotland Escocia
scrambled eggs
  huevos revueltos

scratch (n) arañazo m
scratch (vb) rascar
screen pantalla f
screw tornillo m
screwdriver
  destornillador m
scrubbing brush
  cepillo para fregar
scuba diving
  submarinismo m
sea mar m/f
seagull gaviota f
seasick mareado/a
seaside costa f
season temporada f
season ticket abono m,
  billete de temporada
seasoning
  condimento m
seat asiento m
seatbelt cinturón de
  seguridad
seaweed alga f
secluded aislado/a
second segundo/a
second-class
  segunda clase
second-hand
  segunda mano
secretary
  secretario/a m/f
security guard
  guardia de seguridad
see ver
self-catering
  alojamiento con cocina
self-employed trabajar
  por cuenta propia

ENGLISH → SPANISH

self-service autoservicio m
sell vender
sell-by date fecha de vencimiento
send enviar, mandar
senior citizen jubilado/a m/f
sentence (grammar) frase f
sentence (law) sentencia f
separate separado/a
September septiembre m
septic séptico/a
septic tank tanque séptico
serious serio/a
service servicio m
service charge propina f
serviette servilleta f
set menu menú fijo
several varios/as
sew coser
sex sexo m
shade sombra f
shake agitar
shallow poco profundo
shame vergüenza f
shampoo and set lavar y marcar
share compartir
sharp afilado/a
shave afeitarse
she ella
sheep oveja f

sheet sábana f
shelf estante m
shellfish mariscos mpl
sheltered abrigado/a
shine brillo m
shingle tablilla f
shingles herpes m
ship barco m
shirt camisa f
shock absorber amortiguador m
shoe zapato m
shoelace cordón m
shop tienda f
shop assistant dependiente/a m/f
shop window vitrina f, vidriera f
shopping centre centro comercial
shore costa, orilla f
short corto/a
short-cut atajo m
short-sighted miope
shorts pantalones cortos
should deber
shoulder hombro m
shout (n) grito m
shout (vb) gritar
show (n) espectáculo m
show (vb) mostrar
shower ducha f
shrimp camarón m
shrink encoger
shut cerrar
shutter contraventana, persiana f
shy tímido/a

sick, I'm going to be sick! enfermo/a, ¡Voy a vomitar!
side lado m
side dish acompañamiento m
sidewalk acera f, vereda f
sieve colador m
sight vista f
sightseeing turismo m
sign (n) anuncio m
sign (vb) firmar
signal señal f
signature firma f
signpost poste indicador
silence silencio m
silk seda f
silly tonto/a
silver plata f
similar como, parecido/a
simple sencillo/a
sing cantar
singer cantante m/f
single solo, soltero/a
single bed cama de una plaza
single room habitación para uno/single
single ticket billete de ida
sink fregadero m
sister hermana f
sister-in-law cuñada f
sit sentarse
size tamaño, número m
skate (n) patín m

skate (vb) patinar
skating rink pista de patinaje
ski (n) esquí m
ski (vb) esquiar
ski boot bota para esquí
ski jump salto de esquí
ski slope pista para esquiar
skin piel f
skirt falda, pollera f
sky cielo m
sledge trineo m
sleep dormir
sleeper, sleeping car coche dormitorio
sleeping bag saco de dormir
sleeping pill pastilla para dormir, somnífero m
sleepy con sueño
slice rebanada f
slide (n, photo) diapositiva f
slide (vb) deslizarse
slip resbalarse
slippers zapatillas fpl
slippery resbaladizo/a
Slovak eslovaco
Slovak Republic República de Eslovaquia
slow lento/a
slowly despacio
small pequeño/a, chico/a
smell oler
smile (vb) sonreír
smoke (n) humo m

ENGLISH → SPANISH

ENGLISH → SPANISH

smoke (vb) fumar
smoked salmon
salmón ahumado
snack snack
snake serpiente f
sneeze estornudar
snore roncar
snorkel tubo de
respiración
snow, it is snowing
nieve, está nevando
soaking solution
liquído para remojar
soap jabón m
soap powder
jabón en polvo
sober sobrio/a
socket (elec)
enchufe m
socks calcetines mpl,
medias fpl
soda soda f
soft blando/a, suave
soft drink refesco m,
bebida f
sole (fish) lenguado m
sole (shoe) suela f
soluble soluble
some unos/as,
algunos/as
someone, somebody
alguien, alguna persona
something algo
sometimes a veces
somewhere
en algún lugar
son hijo m
son-in-law yerno m

song canción f
soon pronto
sore dolorido/a
sore, it's sore
duele, tengo dolor
sore throat dolor de
garganta
Sorry! ¡Lo siento!
¡Disculpa!
sort tipo m
soup sopa f
sour agrio/a
south sur m
South Africa Sudáfrica
South African (adj, n)
sudafricano/a m/f
souvenir recuerdo m
spade pala f
Spain España
Spaniard, Spanish
español/a m/f
spanner llave f,
llave de tuercas
spare part parte de
repuesto
spare tyre neumático
de repuesto
spark plug bujía f
sparkling con gas
speak hablar
speciality especialidad f
spectacles lentes m/f,
gafas fpl, anteojos mpl
speed velocidad f
speed limit límite de
velocidad
speedometer
velocímetro m

spell deletrear
spend (money) gastar
spend (time) pasar
spice especia f
spider araña f
spill derramar
spin-dryer secadora f
spinach espinacas fpl
spine columna vertebral
spirit (soul) espíritu m
spirits (drink)
  licores mpl
splinter astilla f
spoil arruinar
spoke (of wheel)
  rayo m
sponge esponja f
sponge cake
  bizcocho m
spoon cuchara f
sprain (n) torcedura f
sprain (vb) torcer
spring (season)
  primavera f
square cuadro m, plaza f
stadium estadio m
stain mancha f
stairs escalera f
stale rancio/a
stall puesto m
stamp estampilla f
staple (n, food)
  alimento básico
staple (vb) grapar
star estrella f
start comenzar,
  empezar
starter (car) arranque

station estación f
stationer's papelería f
stationery artículos
  de escritorio
statue estatua f
stay quedarse, parar
steal robar
steam vapor m
steep empinado/a
steer dirigir
steering wheel
  volante m
step escalón m
stepfather padrastro m
stepmother madrastra f
stew guiso m
stick (vb) pegar
sticking plaster curita,
  parche
still (yet) todavía
still (quiet) quieto
sting (n) picadura f
sting (vb) picar
stitch puntada f
stock (soup) caldo m
stocking media f
stolen robado
stomach estómago m
stomachache
  dolor de estómago
stone piedra f
stop parar
stop sign pare
stopover parada f
store (n) tienda f
store (vb) almacenar,
  guardar
storey piso m

ENGLISH → SPANISH

storm tormenta f
straight derecho/a
straight on siga derecho
straightaway directamente
strange raro/a
strange, stranger (adj, n) extraño/a m/f
strap correa f
straw paja f
strawberry frutilla f
stream arroyo m
street calle f
street map mapa de calles
strike (n) huelga f
string cordel m
striped rayado/a
stroke (n) apoplegía f
strong fuerte
stuck pegado
student estudiante m/f
student discount descuento de estudiante
stuffed lleno/a, relleno/a
stupid estúpido/a
subtitle subtítulo m
suburb barrio m
subway metro m
suddenly de repente
suede gamuza f
sugar azúcar m/f
sugar-free no contiene azúcar
suit traje m
suitcase maleta f
summer verano m
summit cumbre f

sun sol m
sunblock crema para el sol
sunburn quemadura de sol
Sunday domingo m
sunglasses gafas de sol
sunny soleado/a
sunrise amanecer m
sunroof techo corredizo
sunset atardecer m
sunshade sombrilla f
sunshine luz del sol
sunstroke insolación f
suntan bronceado m
suntan lotion crema bronceadora
supper cena f
supplement suplemento m
sure seguro/a
surfboard tabla de surfear
surgery (doctor's rooms) consultorio m
surgery (procedure) cirujía f
surname apellido m
surrounded rodeado
suspension suspensión f
swallow (vb) tragar
swear (an oath) jurar
swear (curse) decir malas palabras
swear word palabrota f
sweat (n) transpiración f
sweat (vb) sudar

sweater suéter m
Sweden Suecia
**Swedish, Swede
(adj, n)** sueco/a m/f
sweet (adj) dulce
swell hincharse
swelling hinchazón f
swim nadar
swimming costume
 traje de baño/bañador
swing balanceo m
Swiss (adj, n)
 suizo/a m/f
Swiss-German
 suizo-alemán
switch interruptor m
switch off apagar
switch on encender
Switzerland Suiza
swollen hinchado/a
synagogue sinagoga f

T
table mesa f
table wine vino de mesa
tablecloth mantel m
tablespoon cuchara f
tailor sastre m
take tomar
take-away food
 comida para llevar
talcum powder talco m
talk hablar
tall alto/a
tampon tampón m
tangerine clementina f
tank tanque m
tape cinta f

tape measure cinta
 para medir
tape recorder
 grabadora f
taste (n) gusto m
tax impuesto m
taxi taxi m
taxi driver conductor/a
 de taxi, chófer,
 taxista m/f
taxi rank
 parada de taxis
tea té m
tea bag bolsa de té
teach enseñar
teacher maestro/a,
 profesor/a m/f
team equipo m
teapot tetera f
tear (n) desgarrón m
tear (vb) desgarrar
teaspoon cucharilla f
teat (bottle) tetina f
teeth dentadura f
telephone teléfono m
telephone call
 llamada telefónica
telephone directory
 directorio telefónico,
 guía telefónica
television televisión f
tell decir
temperature
 temperatura f
temple templo m
temporary temporario
tendon tendón m
tennis tenis m

ENGLISH → SPANISH

tennis court cancha de tenis, pista de tennis
tennis racket raqueta de tenis
tent carpa f
tent peg estaca f
terminal terminal m
thank agradecer
that ese/esa m/f
the el/la/los/las
theatre teatro m
theft robo m
there allí/allá
thermometer termómetro m
they ellos/ellas
thick grueso/a
thief ladrón/ladrona m/f
thigh muslo m
thin flaco/a, delgado/a
thing cosa f
think pensar
third-party insurance seguro contra terceros
thirsty tener sed
this este/esta
this morning esta mañana
this way por aquí
this week esta semana
thorn espina f
those esos/esas
thousand mil m
thread hilado m
throat garganta f
throat lozenges pastillas/caramelos para la garganta

through a través de, por
throw echar
thumb pulgar m
thunder trueno m
thunderstorm tormenta f
Thursday jueves m
ticket billete m, boleto m
ticket collector guarda m/f
ticket office venta de billetes
tide, low tide, high tide marea f, marea baja, marea alta
tie corbata f
tight apretado/a, tirante
tights medias fpl
till (cash register) caja f
till (until) hasta
time hora f
timetable horario m
tin lata f
tin opener abridor de latas
tinfoil papel metálico
tiny minúsculo/a
tip propina f
tired cansado/a
tissue tisú m
to a
toad sapo m
today hoy m
toe dedo del pie
together juntos/as

toilet baño m, servicios **mpl**

tolerate aguantar

toll, toll road peaje m, camino de peaje

tomato tomate m

tomato juice jugo de tomate

tomorrow mañana m

tomorrow morning/ afternoon/evening mañana por la mañana/ tarde/noche

tongue lengua f

tonight esta noche

tonsillitis amigdalitis f

too también

too much demasiado

tool herramienta f

toolkit caja de herramientas

tooth diente m

toothache dolor de muelas

toothbrush cepillo de dientes

toothpick escarbadientes

top parte de arriba

top floor el piso más alto

topless sin camiseta

torch linterna f

torn rasgado

total total m

tough duro/a, fuerte

tour viaje m

tour guide guía de turismo

tour operator operador de turismo

tow remolcar

towel toalla f

tower torre f

town ciudad f

town hall sala municipal, ayuntamiento m

toy juguete m

tracksuit equipo de ropa deportiva

traffic tráfico m

traffic jam atascamiento m, embotellamiento m

traffic light semáforo m

trailer remolque m

train tren m

tram tranvía m

tranquillizer droga tranquilizante

translate traducir

translation traducción f

translator traductor/a m/f

trash basura f

travel viajar

travel agent agente de viajes

travel documents documentos de viajes

travel sickness mareo m

traveller's cheque cheque de viaje

tray bandeja f

tree árbol m

trolley carro m
trouble problemas **mpl**
trousers pantalones **mpl**
trout trucha f
truck camión m
true verdadero/a
trunk (of car) baúl, maletero m
try intentar
try on probarse
tube tubo m
tuna atún m
tunnel subterráneo m, túnel m
turkey pavo m
Turkey Turquía
Turkish, Turk (adj, n) turco/a **m/f**
turn volver
turn around darse vuelta
turn off apagar
turquoise turquesa f
tweezers pinzas **fpl**
twice dos veces
twin beds camas gemelas
twins gemelos
type tipo m
typical típico/a
tyre neumático m
tyre pressure presión en los neumáticos

U
ugly feo/a
ulcer úlcera f
umbrella paraguas m
uncle tío m

uncomfortable incómodo/a
unconscious inconciente
under bajo
underdone poco hecho
underground (adj) subterráneo/a
underground (n, subway) metro m
underpants ropa interior
understand comprender, entender
underwear ropa interior
unemployed desempleado/a
United Kingdom Reino Unido
United States Estados Unidos
university universidad f
unleaded petrol combustible sin plomo
unlimited ilimitado/a
unlock abrir
unpack desembalar
unscrew destornillar
until hasta
unusual insólito/a
up arriba
up-market superior
upside down al revés
upstairs al piso de arriba
urgent urgente
us nos, nosotros/as
use usar
useful útil

usual corriente
usually generalmente

V

vacancy habitación libre
vacation vacaciones fpl
vaccine vacuna f
vacuum cleaner
  aspiradora f
valid válido/a
valley valle m
valuable de valor
value valor m
valve válvula f
van camioneta f
VAT Impuesto al Valor
  Agregado (IVA)
veal ternera f
vegetables
  verduras fpl,
  vegetales mpl
vegetarian
  vegetariano/a m/f
vehicle vehículo m
vein vena f
vending machine
  máquina expendedora
venereal disease
  enfermedad de
  trasmisión sexual
very muy
vest camisetilla f
vet (veterinarian)
  veterinario/a m/f
via vía, por
Vienna Viena
view vista f
village pueblo m

vinegar vinagre m
vineyard viñedo m
violet (adj, n) violeta f
virus virus m
visa visa f
visit visitar
visiting hours
  horario de visita
visitor visitante m/f
voice voz f
volcano volcán m
voltage voltaje m
vomit vomitar
voucher vale m,
  cupón m

W

wage salario, sueldo m
waist cintura f
waistcoat chaleco m
wait esperar
waiter/waitress
  camarero/a, mozo/a m/f
waiting room
  sala de espera
wake up despertar
wake-up call
  llamada para despertar
Wales Gales
walk caminar, andar
wall muro m, pared f
wallet billetera f
walnut nuez f
want querer
war guerra f
ward (hospital) sala f
wardrobe
  guardarropa m

warehouse almacén m
warm cálido/a
wash lavar
washbasin lavabo m, pileta f
washing powder polvo de lavar
washing-up liquid líquido para lavar, detergente m
wasp avispa f
waste residuo m
waste bin bote de residuos/tacho de la basura
watch (n) reloj m
watch (vb) mirar
watch strap correa de reloj
water agua f
watermelon sandía f
waterproof a prueba de agua
water-skiing esquí acuático
wave ola f
we nosotros/as
weak débil
wear llevar, usar
weather tiempo m
weather forecast pronóstico del tiempo
web red f
wedding boda f
wedding present regalo de boda
wedding ring anillo de boda

Wednesday miércoles m
week – last week, this week, next week, a week ago semana f – semana pasada, esta semana, semana próxima, hace una semana
weekday día de semana
weekend fin de semana
weekly semanalmente
weigh pesar
weight peso m
weird raro/a
welcome bienvenido/a
well bien
Welsh, Welshman, Welshwoman (adj, n) galés/galesa m/f
were era/estaba
west oeste m
wet mojado/a
wetsuit traje de agua
What? ¿Qué?
What is wrong? ¿Hay algo mal/malo?
What's the matter? ¿Qué pasa?
What's the time? ¿Qué hora es?
wheel rueda f
wheel clamp cepo m
wheelchair silla de rueda
When? ¿Cuándo?
Where? ¿Dónde?
Which? ¿Cuál?
while mientras

whipped cream crema
white blanco/a
Who? ¿Quién?
whole (adj) entero/a
whole (n) todo m
wholemeal bread
pan integral de trigo
Whose? ¿De quién?
Why? ¿Por qué?
wide ancho/a
widower, widow
viudo/a m/f
wife esposa f
wig peluca f
win ganar
wind viento m
window ventana f
window seat asiento
en ventanilla
windscreen
parabrisas m
windscreen wiper
limpiaparabrisas m
windy ventoso/a
wine vino m
wine glass copa f
winter invierno m
wire cable m
wish desear
with con
without sin
witness testigo m/f
wolf lobo m
woman mujer f
wood madera f
wool lana f
word palabra f
work trabajar

world mundo m
worried preocupado/a
worse peor
worth de valor
wrap up envolver
wrapping paper
papel de envolver
wrinkles arrugas fpl
wrist muñeca f
write escribir
writing paper
papel de escribir

X
X-ray radiografía f

Y
yacht yate m
year año m
yellow amarillo/a
yellow pages páginas
amarillas
yes sí
yesterday ayer m
yolk yema f
you tú
young jóven
your tu
youth hostel albergue
juvenil

Z
zero cero m
zipper, zip fastener
cierre m
zone zona f
zoo jardín zoológico

ENGLISH → SPANISH

SPANISH → ENGLISH

A
a to
a él to him
a la parrilla grilled
a mí to me
a pesar de although
a prueba de agua waterproof
a puertas adentro indoors
a través de through
a veces sometimes
abadía f abbey
abajo downstairs
abeja f bee
abierto/a open
abogado/a m/f lawyer
abono m season ticket
aborto m abortion
abridor de botellas bottle opener
abridor de latas can opener, tin opener
abrigado/a sheltered
abrigo m coat, jacket, overcoat
abrigo de piel fur coat
abrir unlock
abrochar fasten
absceso m abscess
abuelo/a m/f grandfather, grandmother
abuelos mpl grandparents
aburrido boring
acá here, over here
acampar camp (vb)
acantilado m cliff

accidente m accident
accidente de tráfico road accident
aceite m oil
aceite de oliva olive oil
aceituna f olive
acelerador m accelerator
acento m accent
aceptar accept
acera f sidewalk
acidez f heartburn
acompañamiento m side dish
aconsejar advise
acostarse lie down
acuerdo m agreement
adaptador m adapter
adelantar overtake
adentro inside
adiós goodbye
aduana f customs
adulto/a m/f adult (adj, n)
aeropuerto m airport
afeitarse shave
afilado/a sharp
afuera out, outside
afueras countryside, outskirts
agarrar catch
agenda f diary
agente de policía policeman/woman
agente de viajes travel agent
agente inmobilario/a estate agent

agitar shake
agotado/a exhausted
agradable nice
agradecer thank
agradecido/a grateful
agrio/a sour
agua f water
agua mineral mineral water
agua potable drinking water
aguamala f jellyfish
aguantar put up with, tolerate
águila f eagle
aguja f needle
aguja de tejer knitting needle
aguja hipodérmica hypodermic needle
agujero m hole, leak
ahora now
ahorrar save
aire m air
aire acondicionado air conditioning
aislado/a secluded
ajedrez m chess
ajo m garlic
ajustar fasten
ajustar el cinturón de seguridad fasten seatbelt
al aire libre outdoors
al fondo at the bottom
al piso de arriba upstairs
al principio at first

al revés upside down
aladeltismo hang-gliding
alambrada f fence
alba f dawn (n)
albergue m hostel
albergue juvenil youth hostel
alegría f joy
alemán, alemana m/f German (adj, n)
Alemania Germany
aletas fpl flippers
alfiler m pin
alfombra f carpet, rug
alga f seaweed
algo something
algodón m cotton
algodón hidrófilo cotton wool
alguien someone, somebody
alguna persona someone, somebody
algunos/as some
alicates mpl pliers
alimentar feed (vb)
alimento m food
alimento básico staple (food)
aliño m salad dressing
allá over there
allí/allá there
almacén m food shop, warehouse
almacenar store (vb)
almendra f almond
almohada f pillow

SPANISH → ENGLISH

almohadón m
cushion
almuerzo m lunch
alojamiento m
accommodation
**alojamiento con
cocina** self-catering
alquilar let, hire,
rent (vb)
alquiler m rent (n)
alquiler de coches
car hire
alto/a high, tall
altura f height
amable kind
amanecer m sunrise,
dawn
amapola f poppy
amar love (vb)
amarillo/a yellow
amarradero m
mooring
ámbar m amber
ambos both
ambulancia f
ambulance
amigable friendly
amigdalitis f tonsillitis
amigo/a m/f friend
amigo/a invisible
penfriend
amigo/a por carta
penfriend
amor m love (n)
amortiguador m
shock absorber
ampliación f
enlargement

ampolla f blister
amueblado furnished
analgésico m painkiller
ananá m pineapple
ancho/a wide
andar go, walk
andar conducir
drive, go by car
andar en bicicleta
cycle (vb)
andar manejar
drive, go by car
andén m platform
anestésico m
anaesthetic
angosto/a narrow
anguila f eel
anillo m ring (n)
anillo de boda
wedding ring
animal m animal
animal doméstico pet
aniversario m
anniversary
anoche last night
año m year
Año Nuevo New Year
anteojos mpl
spectacles, glasses
antes before
antiácido antacid
anticonceptivo m/f
contraceptive
antiparras fpl goggles
anual annual
anuncio m sign (n)
apagado/a dull,
gloomy

apagar switch off, turn off
aparcar park (vb)
apartamento m apartment, flat
apellido m surname
apenas hardly
apendicitis f appendicitis
apio m celery
aplazar postpone
apoplegía f stroke (n)
apostar bet
aprender learn
apretado/a tight
aproximadamente about, approximately, roughly
apurarse rush, hurry (vb)
aquí here, over here
araña f spider
arañazo m scratch (n)
árbol m tree
arbusto m bush
archivo m file (folder)
área f area
arena f sand
arma f gun
armada f navy
armario m cupboard, locker
aros mpl earrings
arranque starter (car)
arreglar arrange, fix
arrendar lease (vb)
arrestar arrest
arriba up

arroyo m stream
arroz m rice
arrugas fpl wrinkles
arruinar spoil
arte m art
artesanía f craft
artículos de escritorio stationery
artista m/f artist
arveja f pea
ascensor m lift, elevator
asiento m seat
asiento de coche para niños child car seat
asiento en el pasillo aisle seat
asiento en ventanilla window seat
asociarse join
áspero/a rough
aspiradora f vacuum cleaner
asqueroso/a revolting
astilla f splinter
asunto m matter
asunto escrito printed matter
atacar attack (vb)
atajo m short-cut
ataque m attack (n)
ataque al corazón heart attack
atardecer m sunset
atascamiento m traffic jam
ático m attic

SPANISH → ENGLISH

atropellar knock over
atún m tuna
audiencia f audience
audífono m hearing aid
auricular m receiver
(telephone)
auriculares mpl
earphones, headphones
auténtico/a genuine
auto m car
autobús m bus, coach
autopista f freeway,
motorway
autoservicio m
self-service
avalancha f avalanche
ave f bird
avellana f hazelnut
avena f oats
avenida f avenue
avería f breakdown
(car)
avión m aeroplane,
plane
aviso m advertisement
avispa f wasp
ayer m yesterday
¡Ayuda! Help!
ayudar help (vb)
ayuntamiento m
town hall
azúcar m/f sugar
azul blue
azul marino navy blue

B
bacalao m cod
bache m pothole

bahía f bay
bailar dance (vb)
bajar get off
bajas calorías low fat
bajo below, under
bajo/a low
bajo llave locked in
balanceo m swing
balanza f scales
balcón m balcony
balde m bucket, pail
bandeja f tray
bañera f bath
baño m bathroom,
cloakroom, lavatory,
toilet
baño de hombres
gents' toilet
baño de mujeres
ladies' toilet
bar gay gay bar
barato/a cheap
barba f beard
barbería f barber's
shop
barbilla f chin
barco m boat, ship
barra f loaf
barra de chocolate
bar of chocolate
barranca abajo
downhill
barril m barrel
barrio m area, district,
suburb
barro m mud
basta hem
bastante fairly

basura f litter, refuse, rubbish, trash
bata f dressing gown
batería descargada flat battery
baúl m trunk
beber drink (vb)
bebida f drink, soft drink
belga m/f Belgian (adj, n)
Bélgica Belgium
besar kiss (vb)
beso m kiss (n)
biblioteca f library
bicicleta f bicycle
bien OK, well
bienvenido/a welcome
bigote m moustache
billete m ticket
billete abierto open ticket
billete aéreo air ticket
billete de ida single ticket
billete de ida y vuelta return ticket
billete de temporada season ticket
billetera f wallet
binoculares binoculars
bizcocho m sponge cake
blanco/a white
blando/a soft
blanquear bleach (vb)
bloqueado blocked
bloqueo automático central locking
blusa f blouse

boca f mouth
bocina f horn (car)
boda f wedding
bodega f cellar
boleto m ticket
boleto de estaciona-miento parking ticket
boli m pen
bolígrafo m ballpoint pen
bolsa f bag, carrier bag
bolsa de agua caliente hot-water bottle
bolsa de plástico plastic bag
bolsillo m pocket
bolsita de té tea bag
bolso m handbag, purse
bomberos mpl fire brigade
bombita f light bulb
bombones mpl chocolates
bonito/a beautiful, pretty
borde m border, edge
borracho/a m/f drunk (adj, n)
bosque m forest
bota para esquí ski boot
botas fpl boots
bote m boat, dinghy
bote de residuos waste bin
botella f bottle

SPANISH → ENGLISH

botón m button
bragas fpl knickers, panties
brandy m brandy
brillante bright
brillo m shine
brisa f breeze
broche m brooch, peg
broches para la ropa clothes peg
broma f joke
bronceado m suntan
bronquitis f bronchitis
Bruselas Brussels
bucear dive
buena suerte good luck
buenas noches good night
buenas tardes good afternoon, good evening
bueno/a good
buenos días good morning, good day
bufanda f scarf
bujía f spark plug
bulbo m bulb (plant)
buscar fetch, look for, collect
buzón m letterbox, postbox

C

caballo m horse
cabello m hair
cabeza f head
cabina f cabin

cabina telefónica phone booth
cable m wire
cable de extensión extension lead
cables de conexion de batería jump leads
cabra f goat
cacao m cocoa
cacerola f pan
cada each, every
cada hora hourly (adj)
cada tanto occasionally
cada uno everyone
cadera f hip
caducar expire
caer fall
café m coffee
café helado m iced coffee
café instantáneo instant coffee
caja f box, carton, cash desk, cash register, till
caja de cambios gearbox
caja de fusibles fuse box
caja de herramientas toolkit
caja fuerte safe (n)
cajero/a m/f cashier
cajero automático auto-teller, cash dispenser
cajón m drawer
calambre m cramp

calcetines mpl socks
calculadora f calculator
caldo m stock
calefacción f heating
calefacción central
central heating
calefactor m heater
calentador a gas
cooker, gas cooker
calidad f quality
cálido/a warm
caliente hot
calle f road, street
**calle de una sola
mano** one-way
street
calle principal/mayor
main road
calma calm
calor m heat
calzada f pavement
cama f bed
cama de una plaza
single bed
cama doble double
bed
cámara de aire inner
tube
camarera f
chambermaid
camarero/a m/f waiter,
waitress
camarón m shrimp
camas gemelas
twin beds
cambiador m fitting
room
cambiar change (vb)

cambio m change,
exchange (n)
caminar walk
camino m road
camino circular
ring road
camino de peaje
toll road
camión m truck
**camión de reparación
de averías**
breakdown van
camioneta f lorry, van
camisa f shirt
camisetilla f vest
campamento m
campsite
campana f bell
campo m countryside,
field
campo de golf golf
course
Canadá Canada
canal m canal, channel
Canal de la Mancha
English Channel
canasta f basket
cancelación f
cancellation
cancelar cancel
cáncer m cancer
cancha de tenis
tennis court
canción f song
candado m padlock
cangrejo m crab
canoa f canoe
cansado/a tired

SPANISH → ENGLISH

cantante m/f singer
cantar sing
cantidad f amount, quantity
caña de pescar fishing rod
cañería f pipe (plumbing)
capilla f chapel
capital f capital (city)
capital m capital (money)
capó/capota m/f bonnet, hood (car)
capucha f hood (garment)
cara f face
caramelos para la garganta throat lozenges
carbón m charcoal, coal
carburador m carburettor
cárcel f prison
cargar carry, charge
carnada f bait
carne f meat
carne de cerdo pork
carne de vaca f beef
carne medio hecha medium rare (meat)
carne picada minced meat
carné m card
carné de identidad identity card
carnet de conducir driving licence

carnicero/a m/f butcher
caro/a expensive
carpa f tent
carpeta f file (folder)
carpintero/a m/f carpenter
carrera f race (sport)
carrera de caballos horse racing
carretera f road
carretera de circunvalación bypass (road)
carretera en obras road works
carril m lane
carrito para equipaje luggage trolley
carro m car, trolley
carta f card, letter
carta de vinos wine list
cartelera de avisos noticeboard
cartera f handbag
carterista f pickpocket
cartero/a m/f postman/postwoman
cartón m cardboard
casa f home, house
casa rodante caravan
casado/a married
casco m helmet, crash helmet
casi almost, nearly
casilla de correo post office box
caso m case

cassette f cassette
castaño m chestnut
castillo m castle
catedral f cathedral
católico/a m/f
  Catholic (adj, n)
caucho m rubber
cazar hunt
cebo m bait
cebolla f onion
cebollín chives
celoso/a jealous
cementerio m
  cemetery
cena f dinner, supper
centígrado Centigrade
centímetro m
  centimetre
centro m centre
centro comercial
  shopping centre
centro de la ciudad
  city centre
centro musical
  CD player
cepillo m brush (n)
cepillo de dientes
  toothbrush
cepillo de pelo
  hairbrush
cepillo de uñas
  nailbrush
cepillo para fregar
  scrubbing brush
cepo m wheel clamp
cera f polish (n)
cerámica f pottery
cerca near, nearby (adv)

cercano/a near,
  nearby (adj)
cerdo m pig
cereza f cherry
cero m zero
cerrado/a closed,
  blocked
cerradura f lock (n)
cerrar lock, lock out,
  shut
certeza certain
certificado m
  certificate
**certificado de
  nacimiento**
  birth certificate
certificar register (vb)
cerveza f beer
**cerveza de barril/
  tirada** draught beer
cerveza rubia lager
césped m grass
cesta f basket
cesto de la basura
  bin, dustbin
chaleco m waistcoat,
  pullover, cardigan
chaleco salvavidas
  life jacket
champán m
  champagne
champiñon m
  mushroom
chancho m/f pig
chancletas fpl
  flip-flops
chaqueta f jacket
cheque m cheque

cheque de viaje
traveller's cheque
chícharo m pea
chicle m chewing gum
chico/a small
chico/a m/f child
chimenea f chimney
China China
chocar crash (vb)
chocolate m chocolate
chófer m driver, taxi
driver
chupete m dummy,
pacifier
chupetín lollipop
ciego/a blind (adj)
cielo m sky
cielo raso ceiling
cierre m zipper, zip
fastener
ciertamente certainly
cigarrillo m cigarette
cine m cinema
cinta f ribbon, tape
cinta adhesiva f
adhesive tape
cinta para medir
tape measure
cintura f waist
cinturón m belt
cinturón de seguridad
safety belt, seatbelt
cinturón salvavidas
life belt
círculo m circle
ciruela f plum
cirujía f surgery
(procedure)

cisterna f cistern
cistitis f cystitis
cita f appointment, date
ciudad f city, town
ciudadano/a m/f
citizen
claro absolutely, OK,
certainly
claro/a clear, light
(adj, colour)
clase f class, lesson
clase económica
economy class
clavícula f collarbone
clementina f tangerine
cliente m/f client,
customer
clima m climate
clínica f clinic
club de golf golf club
(place)
cobertor bedspread
**cobrar excesiva-
mente** overcharge
Coca Cola f Coke
coche m car
coche comedor
buffet car
coche de alquiler
hire car
coche dormitorio
sleeper, sleeping car
cochecito m pram
cochecito de niño
buggy
cocina f cooker,
kitchen
cocinar cook (vb)

cocinero/a m/f
cook (n), chef
cocinita f kitchenette
coco m coconut
código m code
código postal postal
code
codo m elbow
cola f queue (n)
colador m colander,
sieve
colapsar collapse (vb)
colchón f mattress
colega m/f colleague
colgar hang up
(telephone)
coliflor f cauliflower
collar m necklace
color m colour
colorear dye (vb)
colorete m blusher
columna vertebral
spine
combustible m gas,
fuel, petrol
**combustible sin
plomo** unleaded
petrol
comedia f comedy
comedor m dining
room
comenzar start
comer eat
comida f food, meal
comida de campo
picnic
comida envenenada
food poisoning

comida para bebé
baby food
comida para llevar
take-away food
comisaría f police
station
como like, similar to
¿Cómo? How? Pardon?
¿Cómo estás?
How do you do?
How are you?
cómoda f chest of
drawers
cómodo/a comfortable
compañero/a m/f
partner (companion)
compañía f company
compartimento m
compartment
compartir share
compás m compass
complejo turístico
resort
completamente
completely, quite
compositor/a m/f
composer
comprar buy
comprender
understand
compresa higiénica
sanitary pads
comprometido/a
engaged (to be married)
computadora f
computer
Comunidad Europea
EC

SPANISH → ENGLISH

con with
con experiencia experienced
con fluidez fluent
con frecuencia often
con gas fizzy, sparkling
con hambre hungry
con sueño sleepy
concesión f concession
conciente conscious
concierto m concert
condición f condition
condimento m seasoning
condimento para ensalada salad dressing
condón m condom
conducción a la derecha right-hand drive
conducción a la izquierda left-hand drive
conductor/a m/f driver
conductor/a de taxi taxi driver
conejo/a m/f rabbit
conexión f connection (elec)
conferencia f conference
confirmación f confirmation
confirmar confirm
confundido/a confused
confundir mix up (vb)

confusión f mix-up (n)
congelado/a frozen
congelador m freezer
conmoción cerebral concussion
conocer know
consejo m advice
constipado constipated
construir build
consulado m consulate
consultorio m surgery (doctor's rooms)
contacto m contact (n)
contador m meter
contaminado polluted
contenedor de combustible petrol can
contestar reply (vb)
continuar continue
contra against
contrato m contract
contrato de alquiler lease (n)
contraventana f shutter
control de pasaporte pass control
contundente blunt
conveniente convenient
copa f wine glass
copiar copy
corazón m heart
corbata f tie
corcho m cork

cordel m string
cordero m lamb, mutton
cordón m shoelace
coro m choir
corona f crown
correa f strap
correa de reloj watch strap
correa del ventilador fanbelt
correctamente properly
correcto/a correct (adj)
correo m mail, post (n)
correo aéreo airmail
correo central main post office
correo certificado registered mail
correr run, jog (vb)
corriente usual
corriente f current (n), draught
cortar chop, cut
corte de electricidad power cut
corte de pelo haircut
cortijo m farmhouse
cortina f curtain
corto/a short
cosa f thing
cosecha f harvest
coser sew
costa f coast, seaside
coste, costo m cost
costilla f rib
costumbre f custom

creer believe
crema f cream, whipped cream
crema bronceadora suntan lotion
crema hidratante moisturizer
crema limpiadora cleansing lotion
crema para el sol sunblock
crema pastelera custard
criada f chambermaid
cristal m crystal
cruce m crossing, junction, intersection
cruce a nivel level crossing
cruce de caminos crossroads
crucero m cruise (n)
crucigrama m crossword puzzle
crudo/a raw
cruz m cross (n)
cruzar cross (vb)
cuaderno m notebook
cuadro m painting, square
¿Cuál? Which?
cualquier cosa anything
cualquiera anybody
¿Cuándo? When?
¿Cuánto/a? How many?

¿Cuánto es? How much is it?

cuarentena f quarantine

cuarto m quarter, room

cuatro por cuatro four-wheel drive

cubertería f cutlery

cubo m bucket, pail

cucaracha f cockroach

cuchara f spoon, tablespoon

cucharilla f teaspoon

cuchillo m knife

cuello m collar, neck

cuenco m bowl

cuenta f account, bill

cuerda f rope

cuerno m horn (animal)

cuero m leather

cuerpo m body

cuesta abajo downhill

cuestión f question

cueva f cave

cuidado careful

cuidar look after

culpa f fault

cumbre f summit

cumpleaños m birthday

cuna f cot

cuna portable carry-cot

cuñada f sister-in-law

cuñado m brother-in-law

cupón m voucher

cura m priest

curita sticking plaster

curso m course

curso de idioma language course

D

dados mpl dice

daltónico/a colour-blind

dama f lady

daño m damage

dar give

dar marcha atrás reverse (vb)

darse cuenta realize

darse prisa rush

darse vuelta roll, turn around

dátil m date (fruit)

datos mpl details

de from (origin), of

de moda fashionable

de otra forma otherwise (differently)

¿De quién? Whose?

de repente suddenly

de valor valuable, worth

de vez en cuando occasionally

deber must, have to, owe, should

débil weak

decepcionado/a disappointed

decidir decide

decir say, tell

decir malas palabras
  swear (curse)
decisión f decision
dedo m finger
dedo del pie toe
defecto m fault
defectuoso/a faulty
definitivamente
  definitely
dejar leave, let, allow
dejar encerrado
  lock out
delantal m apron
deletrear spell
delgado/a thin
deliberadamente
  deliberately
delicioso/a delicious
delito m crime
demasiado plenty,
  too much
demora f delay (n)
dentadura f teeth
dentaduras dentures
dentista m/f dentist
dentro among, inside
dependiente/a m/f
  shop assistant
depósito m deposit
derecho/a right,
  straight
derramar spill
derretir melt
derribar knock down
derrumbarse
  collapse (vb)
desagüe m drain (n)

desaparecer
  disappear
desaparecido/a
  missing
desarrollar develop
desastre m disaster
desayuno m breakfast
descafeinado/a
  decaffeinated
descansar rest (relax)
desconectado
  disconnected
descontar deduct
describir describe
descripción f
  description
descubrir discover
descuento m discount
descuento de
  estudiante
  student discount
desde from (time)
desear wish
desembalar unpack
desempleado/a
  unemployed
desfiladero m pass (n)
desgarrar tear (vb)
desgarrón m tear (n)
desierto m desert
desinfectante m
  disinfectant
desinfectante bucal
  mouthwash
deslizarse slide (vb)
desmaquillador para
  ojos eye make-up
  remover

desmayarse faint (vb)
despacio slowly
desperfecto m flaw
despertar awake,
wake up
**desprendimiento de
tierras** landslide
después after,
afterwards
destino m destination
destornillador m
screwdriver
destornillar unscrew
desviación bypass
desvío m detour
detalles mpl details
detergente m cleaning
solution, detergent,
washing-up liquid
detrás behind
deudas fpl debts
devolver give back,
refund (vb)
día m day
día de semana
weekday
día feriado public
holiday
diabético/a m/f
diabetic (adj, n)
diamante m diamond
diapositiva f slide
(photo)
diariamente daily
diario m diary
diarrea f diarrhoea
dibujo m drawing

diccionario m
dictionary
diciembre m
December
diente m tooth
diesel m diesel
dieta f diet
diferencia f
difference
diferente different
difícil difficult
Dinamarca Denmark
dínamo f dynamo
dinero m money
dinero efectivo cash
Dios m God
dirección f direction
directamente
straightaway
directo/a direct (adj)
directorio telefónico
telephone directory
dirigir steer
disco m disk, record
(n, music)
**disco de
aparcamiento**
parking disc
disco duro hard disk
¿Disculpa? Pardon?
¡Disculpa! Sorry!
disculpa f apology,
excuse (n)
discutir quarrel (vb)
disfrutar enjoy
disponible available
distancia f distance
distrito m district

diversión f fun (n)
divertido/a fun (adj)
divorciado divorced
dobladillo m hem
doblar bend
doble double
docena f dozen
documento m
document, record
(legal)
**documento de
identidad** identity
card
documentos de viajes
travel documents
doler hurt (vb)
dolor m ache, pain
dolor de cabeza
headache
dolor de espalda
backache
dolor de estómago
stomachache
dolor de garganta
sore throat
dolor de muelas
toothache
dolor de oídos
earache
dolorido/a sore
doloroso/a painful
doméstico/a domestic
domingo m Sunday
¿Dónde? Where?
donut m doughnut
dormir sleep
dos veces twice
droga f drug (narcotic)

droga tranquilizante
tranquillizer
ducha f shower
duele it hurts
dueño/a m/f owner
dulce sweet (adj)
dulce m candy
durante during
durante la noche
overnight
durazno m peach
duro/a hard, tough

E
echar throw
echar de menos
homesickness
economía f economy
edad f age
edificio m building
**edificio de aparta-
mentos** block of flats
edredón m duvet, quilt
educado/a formal,
polite
efectivo cash
ejemplo m example
él he, him
él/ella/ello it (subject)
el/los the
el piso más alto
top floor
elástico/a elastic
electricidad f electricity
electricista m/f
electrician
eléctrico/a electric
elegante posh

SPANISH → ENGLISH

elegir choose
elevador lift, elevator
elevador de silla
  chair lift
ella she
ellos/ellas they
embajada f embassy
embarazada pregnant
embotellamiento m
  traffic jam
embrague m
  clutch (car)
emergencia f
  emergency
empacar pack (vb)
empanada f pie
empaste m
  filling (tooth)
empezar start
empinado/a steep
empujar push
en at, in, into, on
en algún lugar
  somewhere
en el extranjero
  abroad
en forma fit (healthy)
en los alrededores
  nearby
en lugar de instead
¡Encantado!
  Pleased to meet you!
encantado/a glad
encendedor m
  cigarette lighter
encender switch on
encendido m
  ignition

enchufe m plug,
  socket (elec)
encoger shrink
encontrar find, meet
enero m January
enfermedad f disease,
  illness
**enfermedad de
  trasmisión sexual**
  venereal disease
enfermero/a m/f
  nurse
enfermo/a ill, sick
¡Enhorabuena!
  Congratulations!
enojado angry
ensalada f salad
enseñar teach
ensuciar litter (vb)
entender understand
entero/a whole (adj)
entrada f admission
  fee, cover charge,
  entrance, entrance fee
entrar enter
entre come in
entrega f delivery
entregar deliver
entusiasmante
  exciting
enviar send
enviar por correo
  mail, post (vb)
envolver wrap up
epilepsia f epilepsy
epiléptico/a epileptic
equipaje m baggage,
  luggage

equipaje de mano
hand luggage

equipo m equipment,
gear, team

**equipo de ropa
deportiva** tracksuit

era/estaba were

error m error, mistake

erupción f rash

es/está is

escalera f ladder,
stairs

escalera mecánica
escalator

escalfado poached

escalón m step

escapar escape (vb)

escarbadientes
toothpick

escoba f broom

escocés/escocesa
m/f Scot, Scottish
(n, adj)

Escocia Scotland

escoger choose

esconder hide

escribir write

escritorio m desk

escuchar hear, listen

escuela f school

ese/esa m/f that

esencial essential

eslovaco Slovak

esmalte de uñas
nail varnish/polish

esos/esas those

espalda f back

España Spain

español/a m/f
Spaniard, Spanish

especia f spice

especialidad f
speciality

especialmente
especially

espectáculo m
show (n)

**espectáculo de
marionetas**
puppet show

espejo m mirror

espejo retrovisor
rear-view mirror

esperanza f hope

esperar expect, wait

esperar con ilusión
look forward to

espina f thorn

espinacas fpl spinach

espiral f coil
(n, contraceptive)

espíritu m spirit

esponja f sponge

esposa f wife

esposo m husband

esquí m ski (n)

esquí acuático
water-skiing

esquiar ski (vb)

esquina f corner

está bien all right

esta mañana this
morning

esta noche tonight

esta semana this week

estaca f tent peg

SPANISH → ENGLISH

estación f station
estación de ferrocarril/tren railway station
estación de policía police station
estación de servicio petrol station
estacionamiento parking disc
estacionar park (vb)
estadio m stadium
Estados Unidos United States
estafa f rip-off
estampilla f stamp, postage stamp
están are
estante m shelf
estar be
estar de acuerdo agree
estatua f statue
este m east
este/esta this
estómago m stomach
Estonia Estonia
estornudar sneeze
estrecho/a narrow
estrella f star
estreñido/a constipated
estudiante m/f student
estúpido/a stupid
etiqueta f label, luggage tag
Europa Europe

europeo/a European (adj, n)
evitar avoid
exactamente exactly
exacto accurate
examen m examination
excelente excellent
excepto except
exceso de equipaje excess luggage
excluir exclude
excursión f excursion
experimentado/a experienced
explicar explain
explosión f explosion
explotar burst
exportar export
exposición f exhibition, exposure
expreso m express (train)
extensión f extension
extinguidor de fuego fire extinguisher
extra extra
extranjero/a m/f foreign, foreigner (adj, n)
extraño/a m/f strange, stranger (adj, n)
extraordinario/a extraordinary

F
fábrica f factory
fábrica de cerveza brewery
fabuloso amazing

fachada f façade
fácil easy
facsímil fax
factura f invoice
falda f skirt
falso/a fake (adj), false
familia f family
famoso/a famous
farmacéutico/a m/f
  chemist, pharmacist
farmacia f pharmacy
faro m headlight
fascinante astonishing
favorito/a favourite
fax fax
febrero m February
fecha f date (of year)
fecha de nacimiento
  date of birth
fecha de vencimiento
  sell-by date
felicitaciones fpl
  congratulations
feliz happy
¡Feliz Año Nuevo!
  Happy New Year!
¡Feliz Semana Santa!
  Happy Easter!
feo/a ugly, awful
feria f fair (fête)
ferretería f DIY shop,
  hardware shop,
  ironmonger's
ferrocarril m railway
ferry m ferry
festival m festival
fibra sintética
  man-made fibre

fiebre f fever
fiebre del heno
  hay fever
fiesta f party
  (celebration)
fiesta nacional
  public holiday
fila f row (n)
filete m fillet
film a color colour film
filmar film (vb)
filtro m filter
fin de semana
  weekend
final m end
finalmente eventually
fino/a fine (adj)
firma f signature
firmar sign (vb)
flaco/a thin
flor f flower
florista m/f florist
folleto m brochure,
  leaflet
forma f form (shape)
formal formal
formulario m form
  (document)
formulario de
  inscripción
  registration form
forúnculo m boil (n)
fósforos mpl
  matches (for lighting)
foto f photo, picture
fotocopia f
  photocopy (n)

SPANISH → ENGLISH

SPANISH → ENGLISH

fotografía f
photograph (n)
fotografiar
photograph (vb)
fractura f fracture
frágil breakable
frambuesa f
raspberry
francés/francesa m/f
French, Frenchman/
woman (adj, n)
Francia France
franela f flannel
franqueo m postage
frasco m jar
frase f sentence
(grammar)
frecuente frequent
fregadero m sink
freír fry
freno m brake (n)
freno de mano
handbrake
frente f forehead
frente m front
fresco/a cool, fresh
frijol m bean
frío/a cold
frito/a fried
fruta f fruit
frutilla f strawberry
fuego m fire
fuente f fountain
fuera away, out,
outside
fuerte strong, tough
fuerte m fortress
fumar smoke (vb)

funda para almohada
pillowcase
funda para edredón
duvet cover
funeral m funeral
funicular m funicular
fusible m fuse
fútbol m football
futuro m future

G
gafas fpl glasses,
spectacles
gafas de sol
sunglasses
gafas protectoras
goggles
galería f gallery
Gales Wales
galés/galesa m/f
Welsh, Welshman,
Welshwoman (adj, n)
galleta f biscuit, cookie
galón m gallon
gamba f prawn
gamuza f suede
ganar win
ganso m goose
garaje m garage
garantía f guarantee
garganta f throat
gas m gas
gastar spend (money)
gastos mpl expenses
gato m jack (car)
gato/a m/f cat
gaviota f seagull
gay gay

gemelos twins
gemelos mpl cufflinks
general general
generalmente mostly, usually
generoso/a generous
gente f folk, people
genuino/a genuine
gerente m/f manager
gimnasio m gym
Ginebra Geneva
giro m money order
glaciar m glacier
gobierno m government
golpear hit, knock
goma f rubber
gordo/a fat
gorro m cap
gota f drop (n)
gotas para los ojos eye drops
gotear leak (vb)
gótico/a Gothic
grabadora f tape recorder
gracioso/a funny
grado degree (measurement)
gradualmente gradually
gramática f grammar
gramo m gram
gran, grande great, big, large
Gran Bretaña Great Britain

grandes almacenes mpl department store
grandioso/a grand
granero m barn
granizo m hail
granja f farm
granjero/a m/f farmer
grapar staple
graso/a fatty, greasy
Grecia Greece
griego/a m/f Greek (adj, n)
gripe f flu
gris grey
gritar shout (vb)
grito m shout (n)
grosella negra blackcurrant
grosella roja redcurrant
grueso/a thick
grupo m group
guantes mpl gloves
guapo/a handsome
guarda m/f ticket collector
guardabarros m bumper, fender
guardar keep, store (vb)
guardar en el armario lock in
guardarropa m wardrobe
¡Guarde el cambio! Keep the change!
guardería de niños crèche

SPANISH → ENGLISH

guardería infantil
nursery school
guardia m/f guard
guardia costera
coastguard
guardia de seguridad
security guard
guerra f war
guía m/f guide
guía de turismo guide
book, tour guide
guía telefónica
telephone directory
guiso m stew
guitarra f guitar
gusano m maggot
gustar like (vb)
gusto m taste

H
haba f bean
habitación f room
habitación doble
double room
habitación libre
vacancy
**habitación para
uno/single** single
room
hablar speak, talk
hace una semana
a week ago
hacer do, make
hacer autostop
hitchhike
hacer cola queue (vb)
hacer dedo hitchhike
hacienda f farmhouse

hamburguesa f
hamburger
harina f flour
hasta even (adv), till, until
¿Hay algo mal/malo?
What is wrong?
hecho/a made
hecho a mano
handmade
helada f frost
helado m ice cream
helicóptero m
helicopter
herida f injury
herido/a injured
hermana f sister
hermano m brother
hernia f hernia
herpes m shingles
herramienta f tool
hervidor m kettle
hervir boil (vb)
hidroala f hydrofoil
hidrodeslizador m
hovercraft
hielo m ice
hierbas fpl herbs
hierro m iron (n, metal)
hígado m liver
hija f daughter
hijo m son
hilado m thread
hilo dental dental floss
hinchado/a swollen
hincharse swell
hinchazón f swelling
hipódromo m race
course

historia f history
histórico/a historic
hoja f leaf
hoja de afeitar razor
blade, razor
hoja de laurel bay leaf
holandés/holandesa
m/f Dutch, Dutchman,
Dutchwoman (adj, n)
hombre m man
hombres m men
hombro m shoulder
homosexual gay,
homosexual
hongo m mushroom
honrado/a honest
hora f hour, time
horario m timetable
horario de apertura
opening times
horario de visita
visiting hours
hormiga f ant
hornalla f gas cooker
horno m oven
horrible dreadful
hospital m hospital
hospitalidad f
hospitality
hoy m today
hoyo m hole
hueco m hole
huelga f strike (n)
hueso m bone
huésped/a m/f guest
huevo m egg
huevo de Pascua
Easter egg

huevos revueltos
scrambled eggs
humedad f damp (n)
húmedo/a humid
humita bow tie
humo m smoke (n)
humor m humour
húngaro/a m/f
Hungarian (adj, n)
Hungría Hungary

I

ictericia f jaundice
idea f idea
idioma m language
iglesia f church
igual same (adv)
ilimitado/a unlimited
iluminar light (vb)
imán m magnet
impar odd (number)
imperdible m safety pin
imperfección f flaw
impermeable m
raincoat
importante great,
important
imposible impossible
impresos mpl printed
matter
imprimir print (vb)
impuesto m tax
Impuesto al Valor
Agregado Value
Added Tax
incluido included
incómodo/a
uncomfortable

SPANISH → ENGLISH

inconciente unconscious

inconveniente f inconvenience

increíble incredible

indecente nasty

independiente freelance

indicador de giro indicator

indicador de combustible fuel gauge

indigestión f indigestion

indio/a m/f Indian (adj, n)

infección f infection

infeccioso/a infectious

inflamación f inflammation

inflar pump, inflate

información f information

informal informal

informar report (vb)

informe m enquiry, report (n)

ingeniero/a m/f engineer

Inglaterra England

inglés English (language)

inglés/inglesa m/f English, Englishman/woman (adj, n)

ingredientes mpl ingredients

inmediatamente immediately

inscribirse check in

insecto m insect

insistir insist

insolación f sunstroke

insólito/a unusual

insomnio m insomnia

instalación f connection (telephone)

insulina f insulin

inteligente clever, intelligent

intentar try

intercambio m exchange (n)

interesante interesting

intermitente m indicator

internacional international

intérprete m/f interpreter

interruptor m switch

interruptor principal mains switch

intervalo m interval

introducir introduce, bring in

inundación f flood

inválido/a disabled

investigación f enquiry, investigation

invierno m winter

invitación f invitation

invitar invite

inyección f injection

ir go

ir en coche go (by car)
Irlanda Ireland
Irlanda del Norte
  Northern Ireland
irlandés/irlandesa m/f
  Irish, Irishman/woman
  (adj, n)
irse go away
isla f island
Italia Italy
italiano m Italian
  (language)
italiano/a m/f Italian
  (adj, n)
IVA VAT
izquierdo/a left

J

jabalí m boar
jabón m soap
jabón en polvo soap
  powder
jalea f jelly, jam
jamón m ham
jarabe para la tos
  cough mixture
jardín m garden
jardín de infantes
  nursery school
jardín zoológico zoo
jarra f jug
jersey m jersey, jumper
jóven young
joyas fpl jewellery
joyería f jeweller's
jubilado/a m/f
  old-age pensioner,
  senior citizen

jubilado/a retired
judía f bean
judío/a m/f Jewish, Jew
  (adj, n)
juego m game
juego de fútbol
  football match
jueves m Thursday
juez m/f judge
jugar play (vb, game)
jugo m juice
jugo de fruta fruit juice
jugo de naranja
  orange juice
jugo de tomate
  tomato juice
juguete m toy
julio m July
junio m June
junto a beside
juntos/as together
juntura f joint
jurar swear (an oath)
justo/a fair, just

K

kilo m kilo
kilogramo m kilogram
kilómetro m kilometre

L

la/las the
la mayoría de most
la semana pasada
  a week ago
lado m side
ladrar bark (vb)
ladrillo m brick

SPANISH → ENGLISH

ladrón/ladrona m/f
thief, burglar
lago m lake
lámpara f lamp
lamparita f light bulb
lana f wool
lancha f motorboat
lancha neumática
dinghy
langosta f lobster
lapicera pen, ballpoint
pen
lápiz m pencil
lápiz de labios lipstick
largo/a long (size)
lastimado/a injured
lata f can (n), tin
Latvia Latvia
lavabo m washbasin
lavado de coches
car wash
lavandería f laundry
lavandería automática
launderette, laundromat
lavaplatos m
dishwasher
lavar wash
lavar y marcar
shampoo and set
laxante m laxative
(adj, n)
le it (indirect object)
lección f lesson
leche f milk
leche en polvo
powdered milk
lechuga f lettuce
lechuza f owl

leer read
lejano/a far (adj)
lejos far (adv)
lengua f language,
tongue
lenguado m sole (fish)
lente f lens
lenteja f lentil
lentes m/f glasses,
spectacles, lenses
lentes de contacto
contact lenses
lento/a slow
león m lion
lesbiana f lesbian
(adj, n)
levantar lift (vb)
levantarse get up
ley f law
libra f pound
libre free
libre de impuestos
duty-free
librería f bookshop
libreta de cheques
cheque book
libro m book
libro de frases phrase
book
licencia f licence
licencia de conductor
driving licence
licor m liqueur
licores mpl spirits
(drink)
liebre f hare
ligero/a light (adj,
weight)

lima f file (tool), lime
lima de uñas nailfile
límite de velocidad speed limit
limón m lemon
limonada f lemonade
limpiaparabrisas m windscreen wiper
limpiar clean (vb)
limpio/a clean (adj)
lindo/a beautiful
línea f line
lino m linen
linterna f torch
linterna eléctrica flashlight
liquidación f sale
líquido de freno brake fluid
líquido para lavar washing-up liquid
liquído para remojar soaking solution
lista f list
listo/a clever, ready
litera f couchette
litro m litre
Lituania Lithuania
liviano/a light (adj, weight)
llamada f call (n)
llamada de cobro revertido collect call, reverse-charge call
llamada de larga distancia long-distance call

llamada para despertar wake-up call
llamada telefónica telephone call
llamar call (vb)
llave f key, spanner
llave de contacto/ encendido ignition key
llave de tuercas spanner
llavero m key ring
llaves del coche car keys
llegada f arrival
llegar arrive
llenar fill, fill in, fill up
lleno/a crowded, full, stuffed
llevar lead (vb), wear
llorar cry
lluvia f rain
lo/la it (direct object)
¡Lo siento! Sorry!
lobo m wolf
local local
loco/a mad, crazy
los dos both
loza f crockery
luces delanteras headlights
lucha f fight (n)
luchar fight (vb)
luego afterwards, later
lugar m place
lujo m luxury
luna f moon

luna de miel
honeymoon
lunes m Monday
lupa f magnifying glass
Luxemburgo
Luxembourg
luz f light (n)
luz de freno brake light
luz del sol sunshine

M

madera f wood
madrastra f
stepmother
madre f mother
maduro/a ripe
maestro/a m/f teacher
malentendido m
misunderstanding
maleta f suitcase
maletero m boot,
trunk (car)
maletín m briefcase
**maletín de primeros
auxilios** first-aid kit
malo/a awful, mean,
bad, nasty, poor (quality)
mancha f stain
mandar send
mandíbula f jaw
manejar go (by car),
drive
mango m handle
manguera f hose pipe
maní m peanut
mano f hand
manojo m bunch
manta f blanket

mantel m tablecloth
mantequilla f butter
manual m manual
(adj, n)
mañana f morning
mañana m tomorrow
**mañana por la
mañana/tarde/
noche** tomorrow
morning/afternoon/
evening
mapa m map
mapa de calles
street map
mapa de carreteras
road map
máquina f machine
máquina expendedora
vending machine
mar m/f sea
Mar Báltico Baltic Sea
Mar del Norte North
Sea
maravilloso amazing
marca f brand
marcapasos m
pacemaker
marcar dial (vb)
marcha atrás reverse
gear
marco m frame
marco de foto picture
frame
marea f tide
marea alta high tide
marea baja low tide
mareado/a dizzy,
seasick

mareo m travel sickness
marido m husband
mariposa f butterfly
mariscos mpl shellfish
mármol m marble
marrón brown
martillo m hammer
marzo m March
más more
más allá beyond, further
más barato cheaper
más tarde later
máscara f mask
masculino male
mástil m mast
matar kill
matrícula f number plate
mayo m May
mayonesa f mayonnaise
mecánico/a m/f mechanic
media f stocking
mediano/a medium
medianoche f midnight
medias fpl socks, tights
medicamento m drug, medicine
medicina f medicine (science)
medicina para el dolor painkiller
médico/a m/f doctor
medida f measure (n)
medieval medieval

medio m middle
medio/a half (adj)
mediodía m midday, noon
medir measure (vb)
mediterráneo/a Mediterranean
medusa f jellyfish
mejilla f cheek
mejillón m mussel
mejor better
mejorar improve
melón m melon
mencionar mention
meningitis meningitis
menos less
mensaje m message
mensualmente monthly
menta f mint
mente f mind
mentir lie (vb, fib)
mentira f lie (n, untruth)
mentón m chin
menú m menu
menú fijo set menu
mercado m market
merengue m meringue
mermelada f jam, marmalade
mes m month
mesa f table
metal m metal
metro m metre, metro, subway, underground
mezclar mix
mezquita f mosque
mi my

micro ondas m
microwave oven

miel f honey

mientras while

miércoles m
Wednesday

migraña f migraine

mil m thousand

ministro/a m/f minister

minúsculo/a tiny

minusválido/a
handicapped

minuto m minute (n)

miope short-sighted

mirar look at,
watch (vb)

misa f Mass (rel)

mismo/a same (adj)

mitad f half (n)

mitigador painkiller

mochila f backpack

mojado/a wet

molestar annoy,
disturb

momento m moment

monasterio m
monastery

moneda f coin,
currency

monedero m money
belt, purse

moño m bow tie

montaña f mountain

montañismo m
mountaineering

montar ride

montar en bicicleta
cycle (vb)

monto m amount

monumento m
monument

moretón m bruise (n)

morado/a purple

morder bite (vb)

morir die

mosquito m mosquito

mostaza f mustard

mostrador m counter

**mostrador de
información**
enquiry desk

mostrar show (vb)

motocicleta f
motorbike

motor m engine,
motor

mover move

mozo/a m/f waiter,
waitress

mucama f maid

muchedumbre f
crowd

mucho/a long (time),
lot, much

muchos/muchas
many

mudarse de casa
move house

muebles mpl furniture

muelle m quay

muerte f death

muerto/a dead

mugriento/a filthy

mujer f female, lady,
woman

muletas fpl crutches

SPANISH → ENGLISH

multa f fine (n), parking fine
mundo m world
muñeca f doll, wrist
muro m wall
músculo m muscle
museo m museum
músico/a m/f musician
muslo m thigh
musulmán/ musulmana m/f Muslim
muy very
muy hecho overdone

N

nacer born
nacimiento m birth
nacional national
nacionalidad f nationality
nada nothing
nada más nothing else
nadar swim
nadie nobody
naranja f orange
nariz f nose
natillas fpl custard
natural natural
naturaleza f nature
náusea f nausea
navegación f sailing
navegar sail
Navidad f Christmas
neblina f fog, mist
necesario/a necessary
necesidad f need (n)
necesitar need (vb)

negativo m negative (n, photo)
negocios mpl business
negro/a black
neocelandés New Zealander
neumático m tyre
neumático de repuesto spare tyre
neumático sin aire flat tyre
nevera f fridge
nevera portátil cool bag, cool box
ni ... ni neither ... nor
nido m nest
niebla f fog
nieta f granddaughter
nieto m grandson
nieve, está nevando snow, it is snowing
ninguno/a none
niña f girl
niñera f nanny
niño m boy
niño/a m/f child
no no, not
no contiene azúcar sugar-free
no fumador/a non-smoking
no funciona out of order
no importa it doesn't matter
no puedo couldn't
noche f late evening, night

SPANISH → ENGLISH

SPANISH → ENGLISH

Nochebuena f
Christmas Eve
Noche de Año Nuevo
New Year's Eve
nombre m   name
nombre de pila
Christian name, first
name
nombre de soltera
maiden name
norte m   north
Noruega   Norway
noruego/a m/f
Norwegian (adj, n)
nos   us
nosotros/as   us, we
nota f   note
noticias fpl   news
novela f   novel
novia f   bride, fiancée,
girlfriend
noviembre m
November
novio m   bridegroom,
fiancé, boyfriend
nube f   cloud
nuera f   daughter-in-law
nuestro/a   our
Nueva Zelanda   New
Zealand
nuevo/a   new
nuez f   nut, walnut
número m   number, size
número de clave
pin number
**número de
inscripción**
registration number

número de teléfono
phone number
nunca   never

O

o   or
o ... o   either ... or
obligatorio/a
compulsory
obra f   play (n, theatre)
obtener   get, obtain
océano m   ocean
octubre m   October
oculista m/f
ophthalmologist
ocupación f
occupation
ocupado/a   busy,
engaged, occupied
oeste m   west
ofertas fpl   sale
oficina f   office
oficina de cambio
bureau de change
oficina de correos
post office
oído m   ear
oír   hear
ojalá   hopefully
ojo m   eye
ojotas fpl   sandals
ola f   wave
oler   smell
olvidar   forget
ópera f   opera
operación f   operation
operador/a m/f
operator (phone)

operador de turismo
tour operator
oporto m port (wine)
óptico/a m/f optician
opuesto/a opposite
orden m order (n)
ordenador m
computer
orilla f shore
oro m gold
orquesta f orchestra
oscuro/a dark
otoño m autumn
otra vez again
otro/a other, another
oveja f sheep
oxidado/a rusty

P

paciente m/f patient
(adj, n)
padrastro m
stepfather
padre m father
padres mpl parents
pagadero/a due
pagado/a paid
pagar pay
página f page
páginas amarillas
yellow pages
pago m payment
país m country
paisaje m scenery
Países Bajos
Netherlands
paja f straw
pájaro m bird

pala f spade, dustpan
palabra f word
palabrota f
swear-word
palacio m palace
palanca f handle, lever
palanca de cambios
gear lever
pálido/a pale
palo de golf golf club
(stick)
pan m bread, loaf
pan de centeno rye
bread
pan integral de trigo
wholemeal bread
panadería f bakery
panqueque pancake
pantalla f screen
pantalones mpl pants,
trousers
pantalones cortos
mpl shorts
pantano m marsh
panty m pantyhose
pañal m diaper, nappy
pañales descartables
disposable diapers/
nappies
paño m cloth, duster
paño para el suelo
floorcloth
pañuelo m
handkerchief
papa f potato
papas fritas fpl chips,
crisps, French fries
papel m paper

SPANISH → ENGLISH

SPANISH → ENGLISH

papel de carta notepaper
papel de envolver wrapping paper
papel de escribir writing paper
papel metálico tinfoil
papelería f stationer's
paperas fpl mumps
paquete m package, packet, parcel
par m pair
para for (purpose)
para mí to me
parabrisas m windscreen
parachoques m fender
parada f stopover
parada de autobús bus stop
parada de taxis taxi rank
parador m hostel
paraguas m umbrella
parar stay, stop
parche sticking plaster
pare stop sign
parecido/a similar
pared f wall
pareja f couple
parejo/a even (adj)
pariente m/f relative, relation
parque m park (n)
parque de casas rodante caravan site

parquímetro m parking meter
parte f part, portion
parte de arriba top
parte de repuesto spare part
partes del coche car parts
partido m match (sport), party (political)
partido de fútbol football match
pasa f raisin
pasado m past
pasado/a de moda old-fashioned
pasajero/a m/f passenger
pasaporte m passport
pasar happen, pass, spend (time)
paseo a caballo horse riding
pasillo m aisle, corridor
paso de peatones pedestrian crossing
pastel m cake, pastry
pastelería f cake shop
pastilla f pill
pastilla para dormir sleeping pill
pastillas para la garganta throat lozenges
patear kick
patín m skate (n)
patinar skate (vb)
patines mpl ice skates

patio de recreo
playground
pato/a m/f duck
patrón m pattern
pavo m turkey
peaje m toll
peatón m pedestrian
pecho m breast, chest
peculiar peculiar
pedal m pedal
pedazo m piece
pedido m request (n)
pedir order, request (vb)
pegado stuck
pegamento m glue
pegar stick (vb)
peinar comb (vb)
peine m comb (n)
pelar peel (vb)
pelea f fight (n)
pelear fight,
quarrel (vb)
película f film (n)
peligro m danger
peligroso/a
dangerous
pelo m hair
peluca f wig
peluquería f
hairdresser's
peluquero/a m/f
hairdresser
pena f pity
pendientes mpl
earrings
península f peninsula
pensar think

pensión f bed &
breakfast, boarding
house, guesthouse
pensión completa
full board
peor worse
pepino m cucumber
pequeño/a little, small
pera f pear
percha f hanger
percha para abrigo
coat hanger
perder lose
perdido/a lost, missing
¡Perdón! Excuse me!
perezoso/a lazy
perfecto/a perfect
perfume m perfume
periódico m
newspaper
período m period
perla f pearl
permanente f perm
permiso m licence,
permit (n)
permiso de caza
hunting permit
permiso de pesca
fishing permit
permitir let, allow,
permit (vb)
pero but
perro/a m/f dog
persiana f blind (n),
shutter
persona f person
pesado/a dull, boring,
heavy

SPANISH → ENGLISH

pesar weigh
pescadería f fishmonger's
pescado m fish
peso m weight
petición f request (n)
piano m piano
picadura f sting (n)
picadura de insecto insect bite
picar itch, sting (vb)
picazón itch (n)
picnic m picnic
pico m peak
pie m foot
piedra f stone
piel f fur, leather, peel, skin
pierna f leg
pies mpl feet
pieza f piece
pijamas m pyjamas
pileta f washbasin
piloto m pilot
pimienta f pepper (spice)
pimiento m pepper (vegetable)
pinchazo m puncture
pintar paint (vb)
pintura f paint (n)
pintura de uñas nail varnish/polish
pinza f clothes peg
pinzas fpl tweezers
piña f pineapple
pipa f pipe (smoking)

piscina f pool
piscina climatizada/ cubierta indoor pool
piso m apartment, flat, floor, storey
pista de hielo ice rink
pista de patinaje skating rink
pista de tenis tennis court
pista para esquiar ski slope
pistas para principiantes nursery slope
plancha f iron (n, appliance)
planchar iron (vb)
planta f plant
planta baja ground floor
plástico/a plastic
plástico para envolver cling film
plata f silver
plataforma f platform
platillo m saucer
platinos mpl points (car)
plato m dish, plate
plato principal main course
playa f beach
playa nudista nudist beach
plaza f square
plomero/a m plumber
plomo m lead (n, metal)

población f population
pobre poor
(impecunious)
pocillo m cup
poco a poco
gradually
poco hecho
underdone
poco profundo/a
shallow
pocos/pocas m/f few,
a few
poder can (vb), may,
might
¿Podría? Could I?
podrido/a rotten
polaco/a m/f Polish,
Pole (adj, n)
policía f police
polilla f moth
pollera f skirt
pollo m chicken
Polonia Poland
polvo m dust,
powder
polvo de lavar
washing powder
pomada f ointment
poner put
popular popular
por by, for, because of,
per, through, via
por adelantado in
advance
por aquí this way
por ejemplo for
example
por favor please

por horas hourly (adv)
por la mañana a.m.
(before noon)
por la noche overnight
por la tarde p.m.
(after noon)
¿Por qué? Why?
por su cuenta
freelance
por suerte fortunately
por supuesto
absolutely, definitely
por todas partes
everywhere
porcelana f china
porción f portion
porque because
portaequipaje m
luggage rack, roof-rack
portero m doorman
portero/a m/f
caretaker, porter
Portugal Portugal
portugués/
portuguesa m/f
Portuguese (adj, n)
posada f inn
posible possible
postal f postcard
poste indicador
signpost
póster m poster
postre m dessert,
pudding
práctica f practice
practicar practise
precio m price

SPANISH → ENGLISH

precio barato cheap rate

precio de temporada alta peak rate

precioso/a beautiful, lovely

preferir prefer

prefijo m dialling code

pregunta f question

preguntar ask

premio m prize

preocupado/a worried

presentar introduce (people)

presente present (adj)

preservativo m condom

presión f pressure

presión alta (sangre) high blood pressure

presión arterial blood pressure

presión en los neumáticos tyre pressure

prestar lend

primavera f spring (season)

primer nombre first name

primer piso m first floor

primer/a ministro/a m/f prime minister

primera clase first class

primero/a first

primeros auxilios first aid

primo/a m/f cousin

principal main

principiante m/f beginner

prismáticos mpl binoculars

privado/a private

probablemente probably

probarse try on

problema m problem

problemas mpl trouble

profesor/a m/f teacher

profundo/a deep

programa m programme, program

prohibido/a forbidden, prohibited

promedio average

promesa f promise (n)

prometer promise (vb)

prometido/a m/f fiancé, fiancée

pronóstico del tiempo weather forecast

pronto soon

pronunciar pronounce

propiedad perdida lost property

propietario/a m/f landlord/landlady, owner

propina f service charge, tip, gratuity

protestante m/f Protestant

próximo/a next

público/a public

pueblo m village
¿Puedo? Could I?
puente m bridge
puerro m leek
puerta f door, gate
puerto m port, harbour
puesto m stall
pulga f flea
pulgada f inch
pulgar m thumb
pulir polish (vb)
pullover pullover
pulmón m lung
pulsera f bracelet
puntada f stitch
puntilla f lace
punto m point (n)
puré de papas mashed potatoes
puro m cigar

Q

¿Qué? Pardon? What?
que hace juego matching
¿Qué hora es? What's the time?
¿Qué pasa? What's the matter?
¡Qué pena! It's a pity
¿Qué tal? How do you do? How are you?
quedarse remain, stay
queja f complaint
quejarse complain
quemadura de sol sunburn

quemar burn
querer want
querido/a dear
queso m cheese
¿Quién? Who?
quieto still (quiet)
quincena f fortnight
quiosco m kiosk, news stand
quiste m cyst
quitaesmalte nail polish remover
quizás maybe, perhaps

R

rábano m radish
rabia f rabies
radiador m radiator
radio f radio
radiografía f X-ray
rallado/a grated
rana f frog
rancio/a stale
rápidamente quickly
rápido/a fast
raqueta f racket
raqueta de tenis tennis racket
raro/a foreign, strange, odd, rare, weird
rascar scratch (vb)
rasgado torn
rastrillo m rake
rata f rat
ratero/a m/f pickpocket
ratón m mouse
rayado/a striped

SPANISH → ENGLISH

SPANISH → ENGLISH

rayo m lightning, spoke (of wheel)
raza f race (people)
razonable reasonable
real real, royal
realmente really
rebajas fpl sale
rebanada f slice
recado m message
recalentar overheat
recargar recharge
recaudador/a m/f receiver (tax)
recepción f reception
recepcionista m/f receptionist
receta f prescription, recipe
rechazar refuse (vb)
recibo m receipt
recientemente recently
recoger collect
recolección de equipajes baggage reclaim
recomendar recommend
reconocer recognize
recordar remember
recuerdo m souvenir
red f net, web
redondo/a round
reducción f reduction
reducir reduce
reembolsar refund (vb)

reembolso m refund (n)
reemplazo de cadera hip replacement
refresco m soft drink
refrigerador m fridge
regalar present (vb)
regalo m gift, present (n)
regalo de boda wedding present
regalo de cumpleaños birthday present
región f region
registrar check, inspect
registrarse check in
registro m register (n)
regla f ruler
regresar come back, return
reina f queen
Reino Unido United Kingdom
reír laugh (vb)
relámpago flash (of lightning)
relleno/a stuffed
relleno m filling (sandwich)
reloj m clock, watch
remar row (vb)
remendar mend
remo m oar
remolcar tow
remolque m trailer
reparación f repair (n)
reparar fix, repair (vb)

repelente de insectos insect repellent
repetir repeat
repleto/a crowded
repollo m cabbage
representación f performance
representante de ventas sales representative
República Checa Czech Republic
República de Eslovaquia Slovak Republic
requerir require
resaca f hangover
resbaladizo/a slippery
resbalarse slip
rescate m rescue (n)
rescate de montaña mountain rescue
reserva f reservation
reserva natural nature reserve
reservar reserve
residente m/f resident (adj, n)
residuo m waste
resistente al horno ovenproof
respetuoso/a polite
respirar breathe
responder answer (vb)
respuesta f answer, reply (n)
resto m rest (remainder)

retirado/a retired
retrato m portrait
reuma m rheumatism
reunión f meeting
revelación f exposure
revelado film processing
revés m reverse (n)
revisor/a m/f ticket collector
revista f magazine
rey m king
rezar pray
rico/a delicious, rich
ridículo/a ridiculous
rímel m mascara
riña f quarrel (n)
riñón m kidney
río m river
risa f laugh (n)
rizado/a curly
robado mugged, stolen
robar steal
roble m oak
robo m break-in, burglary, theft
roca f rock
rodeado surrounded
rodilla f knee
rojo/a red
rollo m coil (n, rope)
romper break
ron m rum
roncar snore
ropa f clothing, gear
ropa de cama bed linen

SPANISH → ENGLISH

SPANISH → ENGLISH

ropa de hombre menswear
ropa de mujer ladies' wear
ropa interior lingerie, underpants, underwear
ropas fpl clothes
ropero m cupboard
rosa f rose (flower)
rosa pink
roto/a broken
rotonda f roundabout
rubeola f German measles, rubella
rubio/a fair (hair colour)
rueda f wheel
ruido m noise
ruidoso/a loud, noisy
ruina f ruin

S

sábado m Saturday
sábana f sheet
saber know
sabor m flavour
sacacorcho m corkscrew
saco de dormir sleeping bag
sagrado/a holy
sal f salt
sala f hall, ward (hospital)
sala de embarque departure lounge
sala de espera waiting room

sala de estar living room, lounge
sala municipal town hall
salado/a savoury
salario m wage
salchicha f sausage
salida f departure, exit
salida de emergencia emergency exit, fire exit
salir depart, leave
salmón m salmon
salmón ahumado smoked salmon
salón m lounge
salón de belleza beauty salon
salsa f gravy, sauce
saltar jump (vb)
salto m jump (n)
salto de esquí ski jump
¡Salud! Cheers!
saludable healthy
saludo m greeting
salvar rescue (vb)
sandalia f sandal
sandía f watermelon
sandwich m sandwich
sangrar bleed
sangre f blood
sapo m toad
sarampión m measles
sartén f frying pan
sastre m tailor
se puede romper breakable
secador de pelo hairdryer

secadora f dryer, spin-dryer
secar blow-dry
sección f department
seco/a dry
secretario/a m/f secretary
seda f silk
seguir follow
segunda clase second-class
segunda mano second-hand
segundo/a second
seguro m insurance
seguro contra terceros third-party insurance
seguro de coche car insurance
seguro de vida life insurance
seguro médico medical insurance
seguro/a safe (adj), sure
semáforo m traffic light
semana f week
semana pasada last week
semana próxima next week
Semana Santa Easter
semanalmente weekly
sencillo/a simple
sendero m path, footpath

sendero de bicicletas cycle track
sentarse sit
sentencia f sentence (law)
sentir feel
señal f signal
señal de marcar dialling tone
señal de tráfico road sign
señalar point (vb)
señor m Mr
señora f Mrs, lady
señorita f Miss, Ms
separado/a separate
séptico/a septic
septiembre m September
ser be
serio/a serious
serpiente f snake
servicio m service
servicio de courier/ entrega courier service
servilleta f napkin, serviette
servilletas de papel paper napkins/ serviettes
servir pour
sexo m sex
si if
sí yes
si no otherwise, if not
sidra f cider
siempre always

SPANISH → ENGLISH

siga derecho straight on

siglo m century

significar mean, intend

silencio m silence

silla f chair

silla alta high chair

silla de montar saddle

silla de patio deck chair

silla de ruedas pushchair, wheelchair

sillón m armchair

simpático/a friendly

simple plain

simular fake (vb)

sin without

sin alcohol non-alcoholic

sin camiseta topless

sin plomo lead-free

sinagoga f synagogue

sirvienta f maid

snack snack

sobre above, on, over

sobre m envelope

sobrina f niece

sobrino m nephew

sobrio/a sober

socio/a m/f partner (business)

socorrista m/f lifeguard

soda f soda

sofá m couch

soga f rope

sol m sun

solamente just, only

soleado/a sunny

solicitud f request (n)

solo alone, single

sólo only (adv)

soltero/a single

soluble soluble

sombra f shade

sombra de ojos eye shadow

sombrero m hat

sombrilla f sunshade

somnífero m sleeping pill

son are

sonar ring (vb)

sonreír smile (vb)

sopa f soup

sordo/a deaf

sostén m bra

sótano m basement

su her, his

suave soft

subir climb, get on

submarinismo m scuba diving

subterráneo m tunnel

subterráneo/a underground (adj)

subtítulo m subtitle

sucio/a dirty, nasty

sucursal f branch (office)

Sudáfrica South Africa

sudafricano/a South African (adj, n)

sudar sweat (vb)

Suecia f Sweden

sueco/a m/f Swedish, Swede (adj, n)
suegra f mother-in-law
suegro m father-in-law
suegros mpl in-laws, parents-in-law
suela f sole (shoe)
sueldo m wage
suelo m floor (of room)
suelto/a loose
suerte f luck
suéter m jumper, sweater
suficiente plenty, enough
Suiza Switzerland
suizo/a m/f Swiss (adj, n)
suizo-alemán Swiss-German
superior up-market
suplemento m supplement
sur m south
suspensión f suspension

T

tabla de planchar ironing board
tabla de surfear surfboard
tablilla f shingle
tacho de la basura waste bin
tal vez maybe, perhaps
taladro m drill (n)

talco m talcum powder
talla media medium sized
talón m heel
tamaño m size
también also, too
tampón m tampon
tanque m tank
tanque séptico septic tank
tapa f lid
tapado jammed
tapón m plug (bath)
tarde late
tarde f afternoon, early evening
tarea f housework
tarifa f fare
tarjeta f card
tarjeta de crédito charge card, credit card
tarjeta de cumpleaños birthday card
tarjeta de embarque boarding card
tarjeta de identidad identity card
tarjeta de identidad bancaria cheque card
tarjeta de llamadas phone card
taxi m cab, taxi
taxista m/f taxi driver
taza f cup, mug
té m tea
té de hierbas, té natural herbal tea

SPANISH → ENGLISH

teatro m theatre
techo m roof
techo corredizo
  sunroof
tejer knit
tejido m knitwear,
  material, fabric
teleférico m cable car
teléfono m phone,
  telephone
teléfono móvil mobile
  phone
teléfono pago/público
  payphone
televisión f television
temperatura f
  temperature
templo m temple
temporada f season
temporario temporary
tenazas fpl pliers
tendedero m clothes
  line
tendón m tendon
tenedor m fork
tener have, hold
tener miedo be
  afraid of
tener que have to
tener sed thirsty
tener suerte lucky
tengo dolor it's sore
tenis m tennis
teñir dye (vb)
termas fpl hot spring
terminal m terminal
terminar finish (vb)
termo m flask

termómetro m
  thermometer
ternera f calf, veal
terremoto m
  earthquake
terrible awful
terrón m lump
testigo m/f witness
teta f breast
tetera f teapot
tetina f teat (bottle)
tía f aunt
tiempo m weather
tienda f shop, store,
  food shop
**tienda de alimentos
  naturales** health
  food shop
**tienda de
  departamentos**
  department store
tierra f earth, ground,
  land
tijeras fpl scissors
tijeras para uñas nail
  scissors
timbre m doorbell
tímido/a shy
timón m rudder
tinta f ink
tinte m dye (n)
tintorería f dry cleaner's
tío m uncle
típico/a typical
tipo m sort, type
tipo de cambio rate
  of exchange
tirante tight

tirar pull
tisú m tissue
título degree (qualification)
toalla f towel
tobillo m ankle
toca discos CD player
tocino m bacon
todavía still (yet)
todo everything
todo m whole (n)
todo junto altogether
todos/todas m/f everyone
tomar take
tomar prestado borrow
tomate m tomato
tono m dialling tone
tonto/a silly
torcedura f sprain (n)
torcer sprain (vb)
tormenta f storm, thunderstorm
tornillo m nut (for bolt), screw
torre f tower
torta f cake
tortilla f omelette
tos f cough (n)
toser cough (vb)
total m total
totalmente completely
trabajar work
trabajar por cuenta propia self-employed
trabajo m job

trabajo doméstico housework
traducción f translation
traducir translate
traductor/a m/f translator
traer bring, fetch
tráfico m traffic
tragar swallow (vb)
traje m suit
traje de agua wetsuit
traje de baño/ bañador swimming costume
trampolín m diving board
tranquilo/a quiet
transbordador m ferry
transbordador de coches car ferry
transpiración f sweat (n)
tranvía m tram
trapo m duster, rag, floorcloth
trapo de cocina dishtowel
trato m deal
travesía f journey
tren m train
trenza f plait
trineo m sledge
triste sad
trotar jog (vb)
trote m jog (n)
trozo m lump
trucha f trout
trueno m thunder

SPANISH → ENGLISH

tú you
tu your
tubo m tube
tubo de escape
   exhaust pipe
tubo de respiración
   snorkel
tubo interno
   inner tube
tumbona f deck chair
túnel m tunnel
turco/a m/f Turkish,
   Turk (adj, n)
turismo m
   sightseeing
turquesa f turquoise
Turquía Turkey

U

úlcera f ulcer
úlcera de boca mouth
   ulcer
último/a last
un poco bit
una vez once
uniforme even (adj)
Unión Europea EU
unirse join
universidad f
   university
uno m one
unos/unas some
uña f nail
urgencias casualty
   department
urgente urgent
usar use, wear

utensillos de cocina
   cooking utensils
útil useful
uvas fpl grapes

V

vaca f cow
vacaciones fpl
   vacation, holidays
**vacaciones
   organizadas**
   package holiday
vacío/a empty
vacuna f vaccine
vago/a lazy
vagón m carriage
vainilla f vanilla
vajilla f crockery
¡Vale! OK!
vale all right
vale m voucher
válido/a valid
valle m valley
valor m value
válvula f valve
vapor m steam
varicela f chicken pox
varios/as several
vaso m glass (tumbler)
vasto/a great
vecino/a m/f
   neighbour
vegetales mpl
   vegetables
vegetariano/a m/f
   vegetarian
vehículo m vehicle
vela f candle

locidad f speed

locímetro m speedometer

na f vein

ncer expire

ncimiento due

nda f bandage

ndaje m dressing, bandage

ndedor/a m/f salesperson

nder sell

neno m poison

nenoso/a poisonous

nir come

nta de billetes ticket office

ntana f window

ntilador m fan

ntoso/a windy

r see

rano m summer

rdadero/a true

rde green

rdulería greengrocer's

rduras fpl vegetables

rduras orgánicas organic vegetables

reda f sidewalk, pavement

rgüenza f shame

stíbulo m lobby

stido m dress

stido de noche nightdress

vestuario m changing room

veterinario/a m/f vet, veterinarian

vía via

viajar travel

viaje m journey, tour

viaje de negocios business trip

viaje en barco boat trip

vida f life

vidriera f shop window

viejo/a ancient, old

Viena Vienna

viento m wind

viernes m Friday

Viernes Santo Good Friday

vinagre m vinegar

vinagreta f salad dressing

vino m wine

vino de la casa house wine

vino de mesa table wine

vino medio seco medium dry wine

vino tinto red wine

viñedo m vineyard

violación f rape (n)

violar rape (vb)

violeta f violet (adj, n)

virus m virus

visa f visa

visita guiada guided tour

SPANISH → ENGLISH

visitante m/f visitor
visitar visit
vista f sight, view
vitrina f shop window
viudo/a m/f widower, widow
vivero m nursery (plants)
vivir live
vivo/a lively
volante m steering wheel
volar fly (vb)
volcán m volcano
voltaje m voltage
volver go back, return, turn, come back
vomitar vomit
¡Voy a vomitar! I'm going to be sick!
voz f voice
vuelo m flight
vuelo chárter charter flight
vuelo de conexión connecting flight
vuelo libre hang-gliding

Y
y and
ya already
yate m yacht
yema f yolk
yerno m son-in-law

yeso m plaster
yo I
yo estoy I am
yo mismo myself
yo soy I am

Z
zanahoria f carrot
zapatillas fpl slippers
zapato m shoe
zona f zone
zorro/a m/f fox
zumo m juice
zurdo/a left-handed